CANADIAN SAYINGS 3

1,000 Folk Sayings Used by Canadians

ALL NEW LISTINGS

collected & annotated by
BILL CASSELMAN

McArthur & Company

TORONTO

Published in Canada in 2004 by
McArthur & Company
322 King St. West, Suite 402
Toronto, Ontario
M5V 1J2
www.mcarthur-co.com

National Library of Canada Cataloguing in Publication

Casselman, Bill, 1942-
   Canadian sayings 3/ Bill Casselman.

ISBN 1-55278-425-8

1. Canadianisms (English) 2. Folk literature, Canadian.
3. Aphorisms and apothegms. I. Title.

PE 3239.C374 2004   398.9'0971   C2003-907487-0

Cover Design by: Tania Craan
Composition and Design by: Tania Craan
Printed in Canada by: Webcom

The publisher would like to acknowledge the financial support of the
Government of Canada through the Book Publishing Industry
Development Program, The Canada Council for the Arts, and the Ontario
Arts Council for our publishing activities. We also acknowledge the
Government of Ontario through the Ontario Media Development
Corporation Ontario Book Initiative.

10 9 8 7 6 5 4 3 2 1

for Darren and Jane Hagan

Fidos habere amicos suave est.

CONTENTS

PREFACE

My river of Canadian sayings flows on apace. Here's volume three already, letting us all visit parts of Canada new to us where we may share lively expressions in an easy, relaxed manner. Here are funny quips and impertinent comebacks uttered when Canadians' hair is down and our maple-leaf T-shirts are not tucked in. In these pert snippets of common speech, down-home folksiness combines with sharp humour. Now some would term that combination incongruous, but those who say so don't really know Canadians. For part of how we laugh as Canucks involves both ease and intellect. In any case, such laughter appeals widely to us and it motivates me to keep storing comic bales of folk talk. I'm working on volume four even as I tap this preface out on a cold February day. In fact, so nippy was the morning that when I let the bull out into the barnyard, why that old bull had to trot back into the barn and slip into a warm jersey!

The sayings are rural, urban, historical, up-to-date, and they keep me in touch with Canadians from Togo Island to Tofino. Lloyd Candow of Pasadena in Newfoundland sent me this sly dismissal: "Now there goes a specimen of God's carelessness." Consider this 100%-pure Torontoism said by a parent when a boy's zipper is undone: "The Princes' Gates are open." This saying smacks of 1950s Toronto and is probably entirely local to Hogtown. The Princes' Gates are the monumental entrance to the Canadian National Exhibition grounds. Opened in 1927, the gates were officially inaugurated by Prince Edward and Prince George. That time Edward didn't abdicate his duty. He took the gold scissors and cut the purple ribbon, manfully doing his duty—so unlike his later shenanigans.

"Are you enjoying your first week in Regina? Got buffalo rubbing stones in your pocket?" This was said by a Cree friend to someone newly arrived in the windy city of Regina. Buffalo rubbing stones were large boulders worn smooth by buffalo rubbing against the stones to rid themselves of their thick winter hair and also to help dislodge ticks and fleas. The implication is: so intense is the Regina wind that one needs pockets stuffed with large stones to weigh one down. Otherwise the strong winds will carry one away! The tang of prairie breezes seeps through every syllable of that saying.

From Montreal via Vancouver come two gems of Montreal French and Anglo-Yiddish. Both describe being in the boondocks: (1) Out in *ville de ruches* and (2) *Au fin, au fin, au fin, et puis de bout*. Rahel Anne Bailie wrote me, "I just heard you on CBC Radio, Bill, which seemed fitting, as *Canadian Sayings 2* has been our source of entertainment for the past few weeks on our commute from *ville de ruches* (pronounced ROOKiss, but with an aspirated h) to downtown Vancouver. The juxtapositioning of Yiddish words with *mots Québécois* gives us this saying that makes me nostalgic for Montreal whenever I hear it. As my social circle contains many transplanted Montreal Jews, I hear it a fair bit. *De ruches* means 'out in the sticks,' so, when asked where someone lives, and you want to indicate that they live WAY out in the sticks, you reply, 'Oh, they live out in *ville de ruches.*' The other saying, to indicate how to get to someone's home way out in the sticks (the east side of Montreal could be *de ruches* to some people), is to say that you go *'au fin, au fin, au fin, et puis de bout.'* Translation: 'to the end, the end, the end, then really the end.' That's probably even farther away than *ville de ruches*, but I'm not sure—I never dared go that far!"

You can riffle through dry histories of Montreal until your eyes are like peach pits and not find language of such sweet quotidian reality. That intensely local talk is almost elemental and chthonic. It springs out of the very ground (Greek, *chthon*) we live on and curls around our hearts like warmth from home's fireplace.

Indeed, some of these zingers are so earthy and organic they breach the canons of good taste. But that too is part of humour's duty. Consider the phrase "blowing oysters." It describes a particularly moist blowing of the nose in which nasal mucus traps air and then bubbles of snot form at the nostrils. The nasal artifacts so blown may resemble the glistening innards of a shucked oyster. Phoenix Wisebone of Vancouver writes, "My brother used to say this about blowing one's nose outside without using a hanky or face tissue. This was in the 1960s at a rural high school in Middlesex County, Ontario."

Emunction ought to follow such oysters. Emunction is an admittedly obscure medical term for the act of wiping the nose. The *Oxford English Dictionary* says it was last used in 1684. The poor neglected thing! What wee word could be more deserving of revival? Besides, emunction is sure to stump verbal know-it-alls during a word game. And think of the deft religious pun lurking there. If you had to wipe your nose on your deathbed, it would be an act of extreme emunction.

Some bits of our speech echo back in time, like this Canadian direction: "She'll be up the line a tad." Usually this Ottawa Valley locution means some place is located further west or northwest of Ottawa, well into the Ottawa Valley. It might refer to a survey line, concession line, rail line, but most probably is a direct reference to the fabled Opeongo line, a modest roadway, a settlement road that begins at Farrell's Landing on the Ottawa River. It was planned to end at Opeongo Lake in Algonquin Park, but never stretched that far.

The road, today no more than a pleasant country lane, fades away near Whitney, Ontario. In the middle of the nineteenth century such roads were built to lure pioneers to settle the remoter parts of Ontario. Like so many Victorian lures to Canadian immigrants, exaggeration was involved. For instance, "free land for magnificent farms" was promised to newcomers. How this farming bounty was to occur on the thin rocky soil of the Opeongo Hills remains a mystery. The many ghost towns now drooping sadly beside the Opeongo Road attest to these false promises and to the fact that gung-ho folks tried to farm or provide services for lumbermen but failed, packed up, and moved away forever. Yes, a few Ottawa Valley lumber merchants found valuable stands of white pine in the forested hills of Opeongo. But after the pine had been harvested, nothing much remained to keep people tied to this hardscrabble stretch of Ontario. A reader named Sarah Elvidge of Yarmouth, Nova Scotia, acquainted me with this expression so redolent of pioneer days.

Then we snap back to a harsh present with this bark from Canadian police slang: "He's a circle dot." In other words, he's a jerk. This is current cop talk. If an officer in some jurisdictions is dealing with an individual he deems worthy of the label "asshole," he will make a small circle with a dot in the middle in his or her official police notes. Another officer reviewing the notes will get the message, and if the notes are entered into evidence, the little drawing can be passed off as a doodle. Eventually, this written practice drifted into speech amongst cops of all stripes.

So here I am, serving up another thousand morsels from the bannock of Canadian speech—sprightly, innocent, sometimes salacious, sayings just to laugh at. Let us press forward into the broad, steamy, teeming meadows of fun. If you have shocking or funny Canadian sayings that you have not found in any of my three volumes, please mail or email them to me at canadiansayings@mountaincable.net.

To learn more and sample farther, visit one of my websites listed below. Now please read on and have a laugh on me!

Bill Casselman,
205 Helena Street,
Dunnville, Ontario, N1A 2S6
Canada

WEBSITE:
www.billcasselman.com

CANADIAN SAYINGS 3

arranged in 287 categories

1. ACNE
1. He looks like he got in a spoon fight and everyone else had forks.

2. AGREEMENT
1. Are we all singing from the same hymn sheet?
• This is business-meeting jargon from Bay Street asking if everyone agrees.

3. ALL IS NOT WELL.
1. I feel like I've been eaten by a mountain goat and shit off a cliff.
•   Having a bad day in the British Columbia interior.

2. Rough as a Badger's Arse.
•   This describes being hungover, being totally messed up on drugs, or being quite ugly. I've heard it in Toronto and Vancouver. The expression came from

England where it is still heard. A badger is a tough little burrowing mammal, probably named for the white mark or badge on its forehead. But the simile also draws on a British dialect meaning of badger as an itinerant hawker of foodstuffs, a cheap huckster. If you are broke in some parts of Northern England or Scotland, you are "skinned as a badger's arse." The behind referred to could be the poor huckster or the little mammal. In the Midlands, something good is greeted in schoolboy slang with "That's the badger, mate!" Badger gassing is farting "the rankest compound of villainous smell that ever offended nostril," to quote Shakespeare. In the latest British slang, the badger is mentioned in expressions of praise as well. "Their music is the badger's nadgers," that is, the badger's testicles. The phrase means it is gutsy, great music. Nadgers is a playful slang extension of the current British *nads*, a contraction of the word *gonads*. A bloke with "real nads" has vibrant machismo or strong convictions upon which he acts.

3. Up Shit Creek in a brick canoe.
• Yet another Canadian variant on the fecal stream, this saying is usually heard with creek pronounced *crick* so that it rhymes with brick.

Len Ross, North Bay, Ontario

4. You're up Shit Creek in a chicken-wire canoe.

4. ALL IS WELL.

1. Q: How are you feeling?
   A: Any better and I'd cancel my OHIP!
• Aubrey Hanshaw of Manilla, Ontario, uses this pert locution, according to her friend Julia Fillion of Little Britain, Ontario.

2. If you have ploughed with oxen, married a widow, and never said a bad word, you go to heaven for sure.
• This applies apparently in Finland where the saying originated, but reports from Ontario are not yet confirmed.

5. ANALYSIS

1. A good horse but a poor buggy? You'll still get there.
• Never mind the exterior; look inside for what drives a mechanism, whether it be an automobile or a complex plan of action.

6. ANGER

1. Jesus wept, Moses crept, and God came on snowshoes.
• Manitoban Nellie Gardiner of Souris writes, "By the time you had said this out loud, you forgot why you were angry."

2. He's really going to spit the dummy over this.
• A dummy is Australian and British slang for a teething ring. Think of a grown man in a baby carriage spitting out his pacifier in a tantrum. I heard this in Vancouver and two people in Toronto emailed it to me as a Canadian expression. But of course it is a borrowing, as so many earlier Canadian sayings were—naturally.

3. By tap-dancing, bald-headed Jesus!
• In many languages, blasphemy adds oomph to ire.
  Len Ross, North Bay, Ontario

4. Wouldn't that gallop a goose to death?
• This is an Edwardian euphemism spoken by men in a parlour or if there were young children or ladies present.

5. And they hang pictures!
• John Murray writes, "My wife, Anne, reminds me of this saying when exasperated by someone, often me."

6. She glared as if her nipples had just been bitten off.

7. ANNOYANCE
1. He's got a hair across his butt.

2. That's my name. Don't wear it out.
• This is said to a pest who annoys one by using one's name frequently to try to get one's attention. One is not amused.

    The Billingsley Family, McGregor, Ontario

8. ARROGANCE

1. Who died and made you King Shit of Turd Island?

2. He's a big butter-and-egg man.
• Teresa Sinkowski of Waterford in Ontario writes, "My mother-in-law Gladys Elve uses this one for those who are full of themselves."

9. BAD BREATH

1. I told you to lay off those shit sandwiches at lunch.
• Heard at a rural high school in the mid-1970s in Middlesex County, Ontario.

2. Her breath would knock the socks off a wino.

    Len Ross, North Bay, Ontario

3. His breath reeks like the devil's own arsehole.

10. BAD LUCK

1. You got the luck of a veal calf.

> The Billingsley Family, McGregor, Ontario

2. That guy would lose money going over Niagara Falls at five bucks a foot.
• This has its variant: that guy would lose money falling down a well at five dollars a foot.

> Lachlan Fulton, Saint John, New Brunswick

11. BAD PLANNING

1. They planted their crop before they built their fence.

12. BAD ROADS

1. This rut factory is a bladder-buster.

13. BAD SMELL

1. He'd knock a gull off dead seaweed.

> Len Ross, North Bay, Ontario

2. It stunk like a knob-gobbler's toothbrush.
• A knob-gobbler is one who performs fellatio.

14.   BAD TEETH
1. He's got so many teeth missing it looks like his tongue is in jail.

2. After years of dental neglect, the Wizard of Oz started brushing his teeth. Dorothy took one look and began to sing, "Follow the yellow-brick road."

3. His teeth are so black, when he spits, he seals driveways.

15.   BALDNESS
1. God only made a few perfect heads; the rest he covered with hair.

16.   BEARDS
1. His beard looked like it should be hanging off his balls.

Len Ross, North Bay, Ontario

17.   BEAUTY'S IN THE EYE OF THE BEHOLDER.
1. If one person says you got donkey ears, never mind; if two say so, consider buying a saddle.

18. BIRTH

1. Giving birth is like shitting a watermelon.

•   A contributor heard this unsentimental assessment of the natal moment as she left a Toronto hospital.

19. BLABBERMOUTHS

1. He has enough tongue to lick his own asshole.

20. BLOWING THE NOSE

1. Blowing oysters.

•   This describes a particularly moist blowing of the nose in which nasal mucus traps air and then bubbles of snot form at the nostrils. The nasal artifacts so blown may resemble the glistening innards of a shucked oyster. Phoenix Wisebone of Vancouver writes, "My brother used to say this about blowing one's nose outside without using a hanky or face tissue. This was in the 1960s at a rural high school in Middlesex County, Ontario." Emunction ought to follow such oysters. Emunction is an admittedly obscure medical term for the act of wiping the nose. The *Oxford English Dictionary* says it was last used in 1684. The poor neglected thing! What wee word could be more deserving of revival? Besides, emunction is sure to stump verbal know-it-alls during a word game. And think of the deft religious pun lurking there. If you had to wipe your nose on your deathbed, it would be an act of extreme emunction.

21. BOONDOCKS

1. Out in *ville de ruches*.
2. *Au fin, au fin, au fin, et puis de bout.*

• Rahel Anne Bailie submitted these two gems of Montreal French and Yiddish. She writes, "I just heard you on CBC Radio, Bill, which seemed fitting, as *Canadian Sayings 2* has been our source of entertainment for the past few weeks on our commute from *ville de ruches* (pronounced ROOKiss, but with an aspirated h) to downtown Vancouver. The juxtapositioning of Yiddish words with *mots Québécois* gives us this saying that makes me nostalgic for Montreal whenever I hear it. As my social circle contains many transplanted Montreal Jews, I hear it a fair bit. *De ruches* means 'out in the sticks,' so, when asked where someone lives, and you want to indicate that they live WAY out in the sticks, you reply, 'Oh, they live out in *ville de ruches.*'

"The other saying, to indicate how to get to someone's home way out in the sticks (the east side of Montreal could be de ruches to some people), is to say that you go *'au fin, au fin, au fin, et puis de bout.'*

Translation: 'to the end, the end, the end, then really the end.' That's probably even farther away than *ville de ruches*, but I'm not sure—I never dared go that far!"

3. Don't blink or you'll miss it.
- It's said of a very small town.

4. He's from B.C.
- B.C. here stands for 'behind Coniston.' This local Sudbury expression denotes a rube, a gormless hick, a mouth-breathing yokel, a real country boy. Coniston is a small mining town near Sudbury, Ontario. Now part of Nickel Centre, the place was named after a village noted for copper mines founded during Jacobean times in the English Lake District.

   Denis Tremblay, Ontario

5. You can't call this a one-horse town. The horse has left.

   Ted Brown, North Vancouver, British Columbia

6. Way the hell out in bum-fucked Egypt.
- Some considerable distance from home then, I think we may surmise?

7. He's so country he thinks a seven-course meal is roadkill raccoon and a six-pack.

22.   BOREDOM
1. *J'en ai plein mon petit change.*
•   Literally this means 'I got enough coins,' that is,
'I've had enough of this.'

   Carmen P. Joynt, Nanaimo, British Columbia

2. He is sharp as a drill but twice as boring.

3. He's so white-bread, his wildest dreams feature
Muzak.

23.   BORN TROUBLEMAKER
1. What do you do? Sneak out every night and shit on
doorsteps?

24.   BOTHER
1. That gives me pain where I should have pleasure.
•   It's synonymous for "that's a pain in the ass."

25.   BRAGGING
1. He could shoe a horse at a dead gallop. Just ask
him.

2. I've ploughed more than you'll ever harrow.
• That is, I know more than you will ever experience.
   Steve McCabe, Kenilworth, Ontario

For another bragging expression, see the Canadian Travel *category in this book.*

26. BROKEN
1. Your computer is hooped.
• Patti Moran of Ottawa writes, "*Hooped* is a word I've only ever heard in one place: Powell River, British Columbia. It means totally screwed up, broken, or ruined."

27. BROWN-NOSERS & FART-CATCHERS
1. He's got his nose so far up Fred's ass that, if Fred farted, he'd be blown to Kingdom Come.

2. He has his nose so far up management's ass that, if the boss farted, he'd pass St. Peter.

28. BURPING
1. Were you raised or brought up?

2. That was well brought up.

3. That was brought up better than you were.

> Ted Brown, North Vancouver, British Columbia

29. BUSINESS
1. Business is like a septic tank: the big lumps rise to the top.

> Ted Brown, North Vancouver, British Columbia

30. BUSYBODY
1. Flitty as a blue-arsed fly.
•   A meddlesome mischief-maker or busybody might flit about like a fly on manure.

> Len Ross, North Bay, Ontario

31. BUSYNESS
1. Up and down like Mary's pants at a picnic.

2. Busier than a hooker in two beds.

3. Busy as a dog with six dicks.

> Steve McCabe, Kenilworth, Ontario

4. Running around like a chicken with its head cut off.
•   That is, frantically busy to no certain goal. This

comes from an old practice that a farmer might use to kill a hen. The farmer would chop off its head and let the decapitated chicken run around to bleed it. It's a method of exsanguination more convenient than hanging up by the feet. Some headless hens dash about for three or four minutes. This really scares the hell out of young children.

> Bob Richardson, West Garafraxa Township,
> Wellington County, Ontario

5. You're harder to get hold of than the Queen.

> Phoenix Wisebone, Vancouver, British Columbia

32. CALL TO ACTION

1. Fuck, fight, or hold the light.

33. CANADA VERSUS USA

1. "The *National Post* is so American it should come in a holster."

• This was written by a fine Canadian writer but is worthy of folk status. Lawrence Martin in his *Globe and Mail* column of January 23, 2003, was lamenting the lack of left-wing voices in Canadian newspapers and how the onslaught of right-wing ranters in the *National Post* does not perhaps reflect the centrist majority of Canada.

34. CANADIAN ACQUAINTANCE
1. We've ehed but we ain't shook.
• We have exchanged comments like "Cold, eh?" but we don't know each other well.

35. CANADIAN ADVICE
1. Love many; trust few; and always paddle your own canoe.

36. CANADIAN ARMY SLANG
1. Black Cadillacs.
• These are combat boots. For example, "Our vehicle broke down but we reached our objective via Black Cadillac. That is, we walked."

   Dave Harris, Petawawa, Ontario

2. Don't be a dentist with those.
• "This refers to cigarettes when a soldier takes a smoke out of his pack. Someone will use this expression to suggest the soldier not be stingy like a dentist who takes only one tooth out per visit. Instead, the soldier ought to pass the cigarettes around. I've had this used on me while buying a beer at the mess," writes Dave Harris of Camp Petawawa, Ontario. Of course, if the author as fussbudget may intrude, it would be better not to smoke any of them, since cigarettes are carcinogenic tubes of poison.

3. Seen.

•   Seen is a term used a lot and simply means 'I understand.' Dave Harris writes, "The expression comes from determining arcs of fire in a defensive position. The section commander will gather his group and pick out a readily available landmark on the horizon. He will then hold up his hand and measure left or right, to a smaller landmark and announce the range. It will go something like, 'Tall white birch at twelve o'clock (directly in front) 400 yards, four fingers right at pile of rocks.' The group will mimic his actions and when they find the rocks, they will shout, 'Seen!' It is now used for any conversation in which someone is explaining something to you and you say 'seen' or 'understood.' Civilians (civvies) get totally confused when this comes up in conversation, and they start looking around for what they think you are looking at."

Dave Harris, Petawawa, Ontario

37.   CANADIAN DIRECTIONS

1. She'll be up the line a tad.

•   Usually this Ottawa Valley locution means some place is located farther west or northwest of Ottawa, well into the Ottawa Valley. It might refer to a survey line, concession line, rail line, but most probably is a direct reference to the fabled Opeongo line, a modest roadway, a settlement road that begins at Farrell's Landing on the Ottawa River. It was planned to end at Opeongo Lake in Algonquin Park, but never stretched that far. The road, today no more than a pleasant country lane, fades away near Whitney, Ontario. In the middle of the nineteenth century, such roads were built to lure pioneers to settle the remoter parts of Ontario. Like so many Victorian lures to Canadian immigrants, exaggeration was involved. For instance, "free land for magnificent farms" was promised to newcomers. How this farming bounty was to occur on the thin rocky soil of the Opeongo Hills remains a mystery. The many ghost towns now drooping sadly beside the Opeongo Road attest to these false promises and to the fact that gung-ho folks tried to farm or provide services for lumbermen but failed, packed up, and moved away forever. Yes, a few Ottawa Valley lumber merchants found valuable stands of white pine in the forested hills of Opeongo. But after the pine was harvested, nothing much remained to keep people tied to this hardscrabble stretch of Ontario.

Sarah Elvidge, Yarmouth, Nova Scotia

38. CANADIAN NAVY EXPRESSIONS

1. You're a waste of perfectly good rations.
- Several correspondents remember this from basic

training at HMCS/CFB Cornwallis in Nova Scotia. The main function of Cornwallis was the training of new entry seamen in the Canadian Navy. Due to a convenient political decision, the base at Cornwallis was closed in 1994. It's now an industrial park with approximately 52 businesses operating on site. The only military presences are the Pearson Peacekeeping Centre, Sea Cadet Training during the summer months, and the HMCS/CFB Cornwallis Military Historical Association.

39. CANADIAN POLICE SLANG
1. He's a circle dot.
• He's an asshole. This is Canadian cop slang. If an officer in some jurisdictions is dealing with an individual he deems worthy of the label *asshole*, he will make a small circle with a dot in the middle in his or her official police notes. Another officer reviewing the notes will get the message and if the notes are entered into evidence, the little drawing can be passed off as a doodle. Eventually this practice drifted into speech amongst cops of all stripes.

40. CANADIAN PRIDE
1. Eagles may soar but beavers don't get sucked into jet engines.

Len Ross, North Bay, Ontario

41. CANADIAN REAL ESTATE

1. That property is moose pasture.
• In Northern Canada, moose pasture is swampy land. Moose love to eat aquatic plants. Beware any real estate even whispered to be moose pasture.

   Denis Tremblay, Ontario

42. CANADIAN TRAVEL

1. "I've been everywhere, man,
   From Verner to Estaire, man."
• This denotes a stay-at-home individual who is nevertheless given to geographical braggadocio. The quotation is from lyrics to Hank Snow's hit country song "I've Been Everywhere." Denis Tremblay of Ontario explains: "Verner is a small town near Sturgeon Falls on Highway 17 and Estaire is a hamlet on Highway 69 south of Sudbury. Total travel time between them would be about two hours."

43. CANADIANA

BRITISH COLUMBIA
Salt Spring Island
1. Put on your Fulford dancing slippers.
• That is, get to the wet work where you'll need to wear rubber boots. "I used to live on Salt Spring

Island, B.C. There gumboots or rubber boots are known as 'Fulford dancing slippers' after the south end community of Fulford Harbour where most of the hippies and farmers live," writes Patti Moran of Ottawa.

2. Get on your Vancouver parka.
• It's a light jacket or windbreaker that would be the heaviest outer garment required on the West Coast to ward off usually modest winter temperatures.

MANITOBA

1. They're just Gappers.
• This collective noun was used along the Manitoba/Saskatchewan border. Those on the Manitoba side of the border thought Saskatchewan folk were braggarts. They got back at them by suggesting that Saskatchewan was just a gap between Manitoba and Alberta, and hence, girls in one Manitoba border town called uppity Saskatchewan boys "gappers."

2. Measure it again, Walter Centimetre.
• "When German immigrants straight from overseas began buying up land in the area of Roland, Manitoba, and started setting up farms, they ran smack dab into an entrenched Canadian preference for the imperial system of measurement which they

could not understand. One gentleman in particular always brought his specifications to Dad in centimetres despite repeated instructions to "write it in English." That guy's first name was Walter and this saying came to mean: "check your figures or measure it again, because I think something's off."

Jim Rudd, The Pas, Manitoba

NEWFOUNDLAND

1. I was screeched in.

• That is, I became an honorary Newfoundlander. According to some correspondents, the phrase originated at Trapper John's Pub on George Street in St. John's. Screech itself is much older, although the word meaning cheap Newfie hootch is not attested in Newfoundland before the early twentieth century. One will hear many colourful origins in a Newfoundland tavern, but this term for low-quality hard liquor, often rum, does derive from the drinker screeching after he or she has consumed enough of it. A noun and verb meaning screech in Scottish dialect *screigh* or *skreigh* was also used to refer to cheap liquor. So one has to ask the impertinent question, Could this use have begun in Scotland and been brought to the island by early immigrants?

Ray Bélanger, St. John's, Newfoundland

NORTH

1. After five years in the north, one is an expert; after ten years, a novice.
• This saying, more proverbial than folksy I grant, is nevertheless apt for this collection. It's quoted in John Robert Colombo's *Famous Lasting Words*.

ONTARIO

1. If Canada were getting an enema, you'd put the hose in Windsor.
• This has been unfairly said of many an upstanding community. I received it from someone not overly fond of Detroit's neighbouring Canadian city.

2. Q: How do you spell Ontario to show that it's a sexy province?
   A: Ontari-oh!-oh!-oh!
• Either invented or quoted by columnist Rosie DiManno in the *Toronto Star*, April 13, 2002.

Arnprior

1. Head over to the Braeside Mall.
• This refers to the garbage dump in Braeside. Braeside is a very small village outside of Arnprior.

London
1. More fun than the Western Fair.
• The Western Fair used to be held in London, Ontario, every September.

Sudbury
1. He's wearing his Sudbury dinner jacket.
• A Sudbury dinner jacket is a long-sleeved wool-plaid shirt worn unbuttoned over a T-shirt. "Think Bob & Doug McKenzie at their sartorial scruffiest," writes Denis Tremblay of Ontario.

Toronto
1. The best thing that ever came out of Toronto was the train to Thunder Bay.

Brendan J. O'Byrne, Regina, Saskatchewan

RCMP
1. Q: What is unusual about the horses used in the RCMP musical ride?
A: The horses' assholes are located in the saddles on the horses' backs.

SASKATCHEWAN
1. Yeah, it's Moose Jaw. But we're closer to the moose's brain than the moose's ass. Unlike Ottawa.

Ted Brown, North Vancouver, British Columbia

2. Q: Why is it so windy in Saskatchewan?
   A: Because Alberta blows, and Manitoba sucks.

3. Saskatchewan is so flat you can stand on a rain barrel and see the Gulf of Mexico.

4. Q: Why do birds fly upside-down over Saskatchewan?
   A: Because there's nothing' worth shittin' on.

REGINA

1. Enjoying your first week in Regina? Got buffalo rubbing stones in your pocket?
• This was said by a Cree friend to someone newly arrived in the windy city of Regina. Buffalo rubbing stones were large boulders worn smooth by buffalo rubbing against the stones to rid themselves of their thick winter hair and also to help dislodge ticks and fleas. The implication is: so intense is the Regina wind that one needs pockets stuffed with large stones to weigh one down. Otherwise the strong winds will carry one away!

2. Regina, the city that sounds like it smells.
• A citizen of Regina's rival in hockey, Moose Jaw, sent this one.

44. CAREER ADVICE

1. The toes you step on today may be connected to the ass you have to kiss tomorrow.

45. CAR REPAIR & MACHINERY

• Jim Rudd of Apparatus Maintenance North in The Pas, Manitoba, writes a note detailing one of the classic places in Canadian life where folk sayings were passed back and forth: "I grew up in a small southern Manitoba town called Roland where my father Eric ran the local blacksmith shop. He was a man of great knowledge and wit both within his chosen profession and when dealing with worldly matters. He would not have fit the customer-service mould of today. The customer was not always right and he did not suffer fools easily. Salesmen who came looking for 'The Boss' were invariably sent across the street to see my bemused mother. After Dad passed away, my older brother Bill carried things on in a similar tradition.

"Now, as you might imagine, 'the shop' held great attraction for a small boy. It was dirty and noisy; there were sparks and fire, and an endless parade of men, old trucks, and dogs; there were comings and goings as they picked up and dropped off work at the door. In the years since, though I did gain higher education, I have worked in skilled trades and now am in the electrical field. The language in these workplaces has never been as salty and sharp as I remember it in Dad's Roland shop. Consequently, I received most of my 'language' lessons there as a young boy, much to my Mother's chagrin.

"I always felt that the farmers saved their best material for the shop, just to see how Dad would react."

1. Wow! The bull gear really jumped the heifer shaft here.
• In other words, this piece of machinery is badly broken but I think I can fix it. Jim Rudd writes, "Incidentally, the seeming gender reversal of the parts is likely because the large gear or low gear of a piece of machinery is sometimes referred to as the 'bull gear' or 'bull low.'"

2. Good enough for the girls I go out with.
• What this meant was simple: that is sufficient work done on this vehicle. One could do more and charge more, but this completes the only really necessary repair. This is a variant of an expression that your humble anthologist used to hear all the time while working at the CBC, namely, "good enough for government work."

3. That rig couldn't pull a sick whore off a piss-pot.
• An underpowered truck or tractor earned this condemnation.

4. That part has been around since Methuselah was
a pup.
• A current source for that part may be difficult to
find.

5. It's fucked in a cocked hat.
• The vehicle in question is not repairable.

6. It rode like an Indian pony.
• The vehicle operated for many hours continuously,
without maintenance.

46. CARS

1. Worse than a yard car.
• This refers to a vehicle in rough shape indeed,
a car used to run errands in large scrap yards.

2. It's a beater.
• A junk car that in decades past might have been
called a flivver.

47. CARS IN CANADA

1. If you see a Packard, duck!
• In the late 1940s and 1950s, some aboriginal
drivers owned Packards, in Ontario folklore if not in
fact. This saying hints that natives behind the wheel

were bad drivers. The other racist implication in the joke is that such drivers might throw tomahawks from their car windows at poor, innocent white folks.

Racist sentiment is part of a few Canadian sayings quoted in this book. Such quotation does not mean I approve of this prejudice. But I am recording the way we Canadians spoke, both for good and for ill. The anti-native saying above has passed into the dust of history. I'm content that it lie there, after we have recorded it for the linguistic record. I have been criticized for including a few racist sayings in my collections of Canadian folk sayings. I would remind the seethers of two things said by the Spanish philosopher George Santayana (1863–1952). Many know the first quotation: "Those who cannot remember the past are condemned to repeat it." But George Santayana also wrote: "History is a pack of lies about events that never happened told by people who weren't there." Neither quotation is absolutely true, but both contain enough pith to merit attention.

48. CERTAINTY

1. Is a frog's ass watertight?

49. CHAIRS & SEATS

1. Would you jump into my grave as quickly?

• "My British grandmother uses this saying whenever I jump into her chair while she's away from it," writes an Ontario resident who wishes anonymity.

50. CHAUVINISM

1. Bunch o' flag suckers.

• This apt insult refers to overly patriotic persons, often Americans. But Yankees are not the only chauvinists in this world. Samuel Johnson's perceptive insight into flag-wavers should not be forgotten: "Patriotism is the last refuge of the scoundrel." He was referring to politicians who, when all their other actions and words have failed to move sheep-like voters, can be depended on to toss in tepid slop about love of country "no matter what the country has done."

51. CHILDISH BEHAVIOUR

1. Your diapers are brown. Well done. Now can you grow up?

52. CHILDREN

1. *Un petit tout nu bordé en bleu.*

• 'A little naked something decorated in blue.' "My mother used to say that when as a child I'd ask her what she wanted for Christmas or her birthday. It meant that she didn't really need anything," writes Carmen P. Joynt of Nanaimo in British Columbia.

2. The Princes' Gates are open.
• Your fly is down. The zipper on your pants is undone. This is something a Toronto parent used to say to a boy. It's probably entirely local to Toronto. The Princes' Gates comprise the monumental entrance to the Canadian National Exhibition grounds. Opened in 1927, the gates were officially inaugurated by Prince Edward and Prince George. That time, Edward didn't abdicate his duty. He took the gold scissors and cut the purple ribbon, manfully doing his duty—so unlike his later shenanigans with that scrawny American tart.

3. Are you going to the movies? No? Then quit picking your seat.
• This chastises children wearing pants who are pulling out underwear wedged in the cleft of their buttocks or who are all squirmy with anticipation or excitement.

4. Child: I'm bored. What can I do?
Harassed mother: Take off your socks and pee in your shoes.

5. Go look for a sidehill rabbit.
• To keep children busy and out-of-the-way of perhaps dangerous work, parents used to send Manitoban kids on a quest for this non-existent bunny.

Nellie Gardiner, Souris, Manitoba

6. A silver know-nothing to hang on the end of your dingleberry.
• "My mom, Fern Boomhower, used this saying when we children were pestering her about what we were getting for a birthday or Christmas gift," writes Darren Boomhower of Calgary.

7. Child: Where are you going, Dad?
   Dad: Crazy. Want to come?
• In other words, stop bugging me; it's none of your business.

The Billingsley Family, McGregor, Ontario

8. What a little buggerlugs!
• This is said of a cute, mischievous baby.

9. Little pitchers have big ears.
• Children will listen.

Len Ross, North Bay, Ontario

10. Little snot gobblers!
• That is, bratty kids.

11. I'll paddle your little patootie until it smokes.
· But, Mommy, spanking is child abuse.

12. You buy them books; you send them to school;
what do they do? Shoot themselves and the teachers.

53. CLEANLINESS
1. You'll eat a peck of dust before you die.
·   This advice to clean-freaks means there is no need
to be obsessively dust-free.

2. Go out and blow the dust off.
·   It's a grandmotherly way of saying "Go out and
play."

54. COMPANIONS
1. If you hang around with shit, don't complain about
the flies.

55. COMPLAINT
1. She'd bitch if you gave her a million dollars
because it would be all green and wrinkled.

2. He's like a gull. If he's not squawking, he's shitting.
   Len Ross, North Bay, Ontario

3. Would you like some cheese with that whine?

56. CONFUSION

1. Confused as a Mennonite offered free dance lessons.

• Jim Rudd of The Pas in Manitoba writes that this saying's provenance relates to "a large concentration of Mennonites around Winkler, Manitoba. Most of the sects there forbid dancing for fear it might lead to more carnal interaction. There was a rivalry between the 'squareheads' and the Wasps." Also in operation here is the imputation of being a cheapskate. Throughout history Tribe A has always accused its neighbouring Tribe B of stinginess. Tribe A, of course, is munificent beyond human ken. This saying brings to my mind as well the old joke about Baptists: "Why are Baptists against sex? Because it might lead to dancing."

2. FUBB and FUBIS
The first acronymic adjective means 'fucked up beyond belief.' Imported into Canada during the late 1950s, it appears to have begun in the Korean War among American military personnel. Also reaching Canada a few years later during the years of the Kennedy presidency was the American Navy's FUBIS attitude. The acronym stands for "Fuck you, buddy,

I'm shipping out." The sense is: I'm abandoning you to your own stupidity. Thanks loads, pal!

57. COPULATION

Ought the anthologist to apologize for what he collects? Absolutely not! According to some readers, I should be dragged to the nearest public square, tied to a dipping stool, and given the water torture every hour on the hour until I repent. My defence is the usual one: I'm reporting how people speak, not how you might wish them to speak. If you are among the glum squad of mopers and killjoys who wallow in being offended, do turn immediately after this section to the sayings listed under SEX. If, on the other hand, you are comfortable enough with sexuality to see its funny side, enjoy!

1. To do your Canadian duty.
• This is used playfully by some of our Armed Forces personnel.

2. To make more settlers for the West.
• This joking reference turns up in an early twentieth-century letter from Ontario sent to Fort Gary.

3. Pounding the tundra to check for permafrost.
• Is eventual frigidity suggested in this saying? Who can say?

4. To get invited to the bush party.
• The Canadian metaphorical reference is to a large outdoor shindig held in a woodlot or secluded forest area where drink and debauchery levels may rise due to the isolation. "Bush" is a popular synonym for female pubic hair, for female genitalia, and for sexual congress.

5. To asSerta your manhood or perform the mattress test.

6. To give her a spray with the old Adamizer.

7. To wet the Brillo pad.

8. To caulk the chink.

9. To conjugate the *f* verb.

10. To take a header into the shallow end of the pool.

11. To clean the hair out of the sink.
• Oh dear, there seem to be a very large number of domestic metaphors for the sex act.

12. To get nooky in the cranny.

13. To take a dive in the dark.

14. To get a bellyful of marrow pudding.
• Here is one of the few salty expressions describing the sex act from a female perspective. It is British in origin and almost two hundred years old.

15. To get hulled between wind and water.
• The Royal Navy is the origin of this oldie, although it's from the female perspective.

16. To get Jack into the orchard.

17. To dance the married officer's jig.
• This too is of obvious military provenance.

18. To get your leather stretched.

19. To give standing room only in the lobby.

20. To receive your bushranger's certificate.

21. To do the bedspring polka.

22. To have a bit of giblet pie.

23. To have live sausage for supper.

24. To play "hide the salami."

25. To rock the canoe.

26. To see if the beaver still needs the log.

27. Time to oil the hinges on the old fur purse.

28. Taking old one-eye to the optometrist.
•   The copulatory hour has arrived. These two synonyms (27, 28) for having sexual intercourse are heard across our Prairies.

> Bill Turner, Brandon, Manitoba

58.   COUGHING

1. He was hawking up lungers.

> Len Ross, North Bay, Ontario

59.   COUNTRY VERSUS CITY

This is not a saying. It's a joke sent in by a reader. But I liked it.

Some Ontario sheep farmers had a problem: every herd was dwindling because bush foxes were taking lambs every night. So the sheep farmers brought in an expert from the city to do a study and tell them what they could do to solve the fox problem. Two weeks passed by and the expert called a town meeting to tell the farmers the solution to their sheep–fox problem. The expert went into precise detail, noting that the foxes outnumbered the sheep two to one. Instead of shooting the foxes, he advised that they should capture, neuter, and release the foxes. Thereby, he concluded, the population would gradually grow extinct and the problem would correct itself. An older farmer at the back of the room stood up and addressed the expert: "I don't think you got a good handle on what exactly is going on around these parts. The foxes are killing our sheep, not fucking them."

60. CRAZINESS
1. You're as crazy as a parrot eating stick candy!
• But what does this mean? Why would the parrot be crazy?

61. CROOKS & SLEAZOIDS
1. He's so crooked when he dies, they won't bury him, they'll screw him into the ground.

    Jim Rudd, The Pas, Manitoba

62. CRYBABY
1. He's a real tear bag.

63. DADDY WAS A DRUNK.
1. He wasn't born, just squeezed out of a bartender's rag.

64. DAMAGE
1. The arse is tore right out of her.
• This expression, popular in our Maritimes, signifies something wrecked, broken beyond repair, seriously damaged.

   Bill Turner, Brandon, Manitoba

65. DANCING
1. I'll dance—if somebody is shooting at my feet.

   Len Ross, North Bay, Ontario

66. DARKNESS
1. Dark as the inside of Toby's arse.

67. DAYDREAMING
1. Sometimes he just steps out for a while.
• He's daydreaming or has lost focus momentarily on what is happening.

68. DEATH

1. He up and crossed the long swamp.

   Len Ross, North Bay, Ontario

2. She's entered the pine-box derby.

69. DEFECATION & URINATION

1. I'm going to shake hands with the unemployed.
• A male is going to urinate and is perhaps bemoaning his current lack of sexual outlets.

   Bob Richardson, West Garafraxa Township,
   Wellington County, Ontario

2. I'm dropping some friends off at the pool.
• This is a typically Canadian euphemistic announcement of a trip to the toilet.

   Martin Cristopher, Springside, Saskatchewan

3. I gotta go shake the grates.

   Steve McCabe, Kenilworth, Ontario

4. I have to go bleed the weasel.
• I need to urinate.

   Glenn Froh, of Lethbridge, Alberta; Guelph, Ontario;
   and Weyburn, Saskatchewan

5. I have to pee so bad my eyes are yellow.

   Dawn Rusnak, Delhi, Ontario

6. Go when you can, not when you have to.
• This advice to children reminds them that every place doesn't have a convenient bathroom.

Hal B. O'Neil, Edmonton, Alberta

70. DEPARTURE
1. Time to make like a fetus and head out.
• "A friend of mine in Renfrew, Phil Lambert, often uses the phrase," writes Nick Smith from Manitoba.

71. DETERMINATION
1. Here's me head; me arse is coming.
• This saying, perhaps Irish in origin, describes someone with a purposeful stride or intent.

72. DIARRHEA
1. He's got more stools than Chairman Mills.
• This Toronto expression refers to a local chair-rental company.

2. He's got the Aztec Foxtrot.

73. DIFFICULTY
1. It's like putting socks on a rooster.

• This expression to describe a near-impossible task involves recognition of the rooster's talons or spurs, which would make donning socks rather tricky.

Bill Turner, Brandon, Manitoba

2. I'm going to a donkey barbeque and I'm bringing the ass.

• A person is getting into a situation that may be impossible to handle. One says this having agreed to do something one knows is quite foolish.

74. DISAPPEARANCE

1. Gone like a sauna bath's arse print.

75. DISCIPLINE

1. I'll make the joy bells of your arse ring.

• A sound thwacking is coming your way.

76. DISHONESTY

1. He's slicker than dual carburetors on a pig's arse.

Tom Lowe, Moosinin, Saskatchewan.

77. DISMISSAL

1. He's all Stampede hat and no cattle.

• This Alberta put-down is heard throughout the year.

2. Oh wow, dude! Can I be you for a day?
• After a high-school hotshot burned rubber in his first car, a savvy girl whom he was trying to impress turned him down with this sarcastic dismissal.

3. Make like a federal Tory and disappear.

4. Make like a beaver and "work it!"

5. Make like Chrétien and "geah ouwa" here.

6. Make like a Canadian passport photo and stop smiling.

7. Make like an Ontario nuclear plant and shut down.

8. Make like a maple leaf and drop off.

9. Make like an amoeba and split.

10. That sucks the Royal wang big time.
• *Wang* is a penis and *big time* is an adverbial intensifier. This shocking statement actually implies that fellatio might occur in a palatial setting. Heaven forfend! But it means that there could be nothing

worse than what the speaker has been forced to
contemplate or propose.

11. Hey, quiz time! Rearrange these two words into
a well-known phrase: off fuck.

12. You're so low you could kiss a June bug's dick
without bending a knee.

13. Up your shit chute with a Roto-Rooter!

14. Up your brown with an open umbrella!

15. The best part of him ran down his father's leg.
    Martin Cristopher, Springside, Saskatchewan

16. You kill it and I'll drag it behind the shed.
•   If two guys were being bugged by an obvious loser,
this threat might be spoken aloud between them.
    Lloyd Candow, Pasadena, Newfoundland

17. You are a nit on the nut of a gnat.
    R.S. (Dick) Heggs, Okanagan Valley, British Columbia

18. He should be shot with a ball of his own shit.

19. Now there's a specimen of God's carelessness.
    Lloyd Candow, Pasadena, Newfoundland

20. Go crawl in a hole and pull it in behind you.
   Len Ross, North Bay, Ontario

21. Why don't you bite my left tit?
   Len Ross, North Bay, Ontario

22. Up your geegee with a wire brush.
•   Both gs are hard. Geegee in common parlance
can be either an anus or a vagina.
Variant: Up yer geegee with a ten-foot pole.

23. Go take a flying fuck at a rolling donut.
   Jim Rudd, The Pas, Manitoba

24. Put an egg in your shoe and beat it.
•   In other words, walk away quickly. Get lost!

25. I wish all your teeth would fall out except one,
so you could still have a toothache.
•   This saying may be of Japanese origin.

26. Make like a hockey player and get the puck out
of here.

27. Make like a self-reflexive suppository and stick
yourself up your own ass.

28. Make like a hotel guest and check out.

BILL CASSELMAN

29. Make like dandruff and flake off.

30. Make like a dodo bird and become extinct.

31. You're such a shit, when you go past the bathroom the toilet flushes.

32. If I promise to miss you, will you go away?

33. You are about as welcome as a condom machine in the Vatican.

34. There's a train leaving in an hour. Be under it.

35. Go fart peas at the moon.

36. If I throw a stick, will you chase it and go away?

78. DISORGANIZED
1. She couldn't run a two-car funeral down a one-way street.

   Linda Mayberry

79. DOGS
1. Blowing an *O*.
• Phoenix Wisebone writes, "In the 1960s in

Middlesex County in Ontario we used to say this about our dog whenever she began to howl. The O was the shape of her lips."

80. DRINKING ALCOHOL

1. I'm a hurtin' Albertan.
• This tipsy lament airs frequently in Calgary around Stampede time.

    Christopher Melsted, Banff, Alberta.

2. Ground swell seems pretty rough tonight, or am I pissed?

3. He was gooned out of his tree.
• Laurel Rice of Dryden, Ontario, former resident of Squamish, reports that the youth of Squamish, B.C., use this to mean: he was so drunk he could barely stand up.

4. He's long gone to Mancoda.
• It's a Saskatchewan expression meaning he's drunk by now. Mancoda was a cattle-buying-and-selling centre in Saskatchewan. After getting the money for his herd, a cowman might well think he deserved a few pints in a Mancoda tavern or beverage room.

5. Drink up and drown.
• Christopher Melsted writes from Banff, Alberta: "This is said to fellow drinkers when last call has sounded and it's time to leave a particular establishment. It's heard all over Saskatoon and I've heard it in Calgary and Edmonton. It might originate in a song by the Saskatoon-based band The Northern Pikes. In the mid-1980s they had a hit entitled 'Teenland' whose lyrics contain the expression."

6. Booze artist? He'd lick it off a leg sore.
Variant: He would drink it off a sore leg.

7. He's drunker than a rodeo goat.

8. He is a wine expert—he doesn't cut his nose by sniffing the cap.

Brendan J. O'Byrne, Regina, Saskatchewan

9. Vitamin P.
Barley sandwich.
Uncle Pil.
• In Edmonton, Pilsner beer is known by all three nicknames.

Richard Wirsta, Edmonton, Alberta

10. He's got his beer goggles on.
• He can soon be accurately labelled blind drunk.

11. I feel like a noodle.
• "I lived in China many years ago and one evening after a few drinks one of our Canadian guests said this implying that she had been drinking too much," emails Carmen P. Joynt of Nanaimo, British Columbia.

12. A bottle of Goof.
• It's a bottle of very cheap wine.

13. Dancing with the Black Death.
• A drinker who gets sick on cheap black rum does this dance.

14. He'd get drunk sniffing a beer cap.
• His alcohol-tolerance level is dropping.

81. DRIVERS
1. Road turd.
• This is a slow driver who habitually drives in the fast and passing lanes instead of where he belongs, in the slow lane.

82. DRUG PROBLEMS
1. He's mainlining with Clorox to get like totally, finally clean.

2. The going got weird, and he turned pro.

3. She thinks private enterprise means owning a personal starship.

4. Gloria's a pioneer. She spent a decade on the leading edge of drug experimentation.

83. EDUCATION
1. Get your education. It's easy to carry around.

84. EFFICIENCY
1. He puts the puck in the net.

2. I'll be all over that like ugly on a moose.

85. ELEVATORS
These anecdotes are not strictly Canadian sayings, but they were spoken to a Canadian. Hey, it's a flimsy excuse for inclusion in the book, but—guess what, nitpickers?—it's author's choice here!

Foreign elevators see me coming. When I enter elevators in sultry locales, they seize; they stutter to a bumpy halt; they choke; they succumb to EVAs (elevator vascular accidents); yes, they stroke out, usually between the twentieth and twenty-first floors. I imagine elevators, cold and steely in their tidy ranks along a lobby wall whispering to one another as I timidly approach, "Pssst, dude, look at that fat chump in the Tommy Bahama silk shirt. Yeah, it's Casselman again. Let's stop dead just when he reaches the sixth floor. Heh-heh-heh." Then a more otherworldly laugh compounded of snapping cable noises and approaching ambulance sirens emanates from their bloodstained shafts.

Elevators flummox me too with operating buttons bearing strange labels. My favourite was the Danish elevator that had a large green push button. Stamped on it in capital letters was the word *FART*. One was understandably hesitant to press down on such a button, out of consideration for other people in the elevator. How was I to know that *fart* means 'go' in Danish?

In the North African country of Morocco at the truly magnificent Mamounia Hotel in Marrakech, one treads the very "foot sands" of the Sahara. One sips mint tea on a palm-fringed balcony, smells the wind-wafted sugar of ripening dates asway in groves nearby, hears muffled thuds of drums of dancing desert tribes drifting to one's table from the Djemaa el Fna, the great marketplace of Marrakech. But during every morning of my two-week stay, the elevator in the main lobby of the Mamounia was broken. And every morning I would ask in my broken Arabic, "Is it working this morning, Hamid?" And Hamid would reply, "No, sir, the elevator is still inhabited by a spiteful jinni. And management has not seen fit to exorcise this jinni. They themselves are incapable of exorcism, sir. Only the wise men of the dunes know the words. And management will not permit them in the hotel, for they reek of camel."

Far more piquant than the haunted elevator of Marrakech was the Mexican one. I visited Cancun very early in its career as an instant resort, in the early 1970s. Tall, American-style resort hotels were just beginning their ugly Mexican hat dance along the Cancun shoreline. Some of the hotel buildings were barely finished when rapacious tour operators began stuffing gullible tourists into half-completed suites. You know the kind of joint I mean, one where exposed wiring has been disguised as handrails. The morning I checked in at the swanky faux-marble desk of fabulous Gringo Muerto Towers, I was given a room on the seventh floor. I was welcomed profusely and then told that the elevator was broken. I would be pleased to take the stairs four times a day. There was a pleasant elderly gentleman in charge of ushering passengers into and out of the elevator, when it worked. Let's call him Pedro. We became well acquainted. Every morning, huffing and puffing from the many tall steps, I would humbly ask Pedro in my probably bizarre Spanish, *"¿E hoy funciona el elevador?"* Does the elevator work today? *"No, señor, lo siento mucho."* 'No, sir, very sorry. After ten days, even Pedro began to lose his cool. He had by then been asked the question four hundred times. On the eleventh morning of my stay, I came down the stairwell once again and emerged into the lobby, a bit cheesed off after a night of fitful sleep.

"¿E hoy funciona el elevador?" I asked.

"No," said Pedro.

"¡O Madre de Dios! ¿Porque?"

Pedro's face scrinched up into a wizened prune of rage and he spat out under his breath, *"¿Porque? ¡Porque la chingante chinga está chingada!"*

In one of the most astute summations ever uttered of the frustrating relationship between human being and broken machine, Pedro had said, "Why won't the elevator work? Because the fucking fuck is fucked."

86. EXCLAMATIONS
1. Suck back, dude!
- One could as well say, "Holy Moley!"

  Len Ross, North Bay, Ontario

2. Isn't that a turr!
• This Ottawa Valley expression is a local version of "Isn't that a terrible thing!"

> Sarah Elvidge, Yarmouth, Nova Scotia

3. Jumping Jesus on a pogo stick!

87. EXPERTISE

1. He's a real connoisseur—mostly sewer, with a touch of con.

> Hal B. O'Neil, Edmonton, Alberta

88. FAILURE

1. Résumé of applicant for a circus job: Can't sing; can't dance; too fat to fly.
• Low self-esteem motivates this delineation of limited capabilities.

89. FAIRNESS

1. Whatever you think is fair—just like Eaton's.
• "When asked to make a decision about something they really didn't care about, both my grandfather and father would reply with this phrase," writes Barb Andrew of Brandon, Manitoba. The reference is to a now defunct Canadian department store chain

founded by Timothy Eaton, one of whose sale slogans resembled this phrase.

90. THE FAIR SEX
1. I'd rather watch her climb stairs than pour maple syrup on a pancake.

91. FAMILY RESEMBLANCE
1. He looks so much like him, you'd think he'd shit him.
• This was heard in the Miramichi district of New Brunswick.

92. FAREWELLS
1. See ya; wouldn't wanna be ya.
   Len Ross, North Bay, Ontario

93. FARM WORK
1. Plough deep while sluggards sleep
   And you'll have corn to sell and keep.
• This old rhyme suggests that turning over a field at night before you plant a crop of corn will increase the yield. Is it based on cogent agricultural statistics?

94. FASHION & DRESS
1. You can paint a barn black but it's still a barn.
•   Yes, black is slimming, but not if you weigh 400 pounds.

95. FATNESS
Our contempt for obesity oozes through these sayings, at a time when Canadians have never been so fat. Is there a connection between the nastiness of recent fat jokes and this growing health problem? You bet!

1. He was so big the hole in his arse weighed 10 pounds.
•   Ken MacKenzie writes: "My grandfather, A.J. MacKenzie of Antigonish in Nova Scotia, was talking about this man who came by for a visit. Apparently this was a very big guy. I remember Grandpa telling how he'd sit on a couch. Then he'd be about halfway to sitting down and he'd just fall and hit that couch so hard you could feel the floor shake. When I was about ten years old, that was amusing. Being a science teacher today, I think it's funnier. After all, as they might even ask in physics, 'How heavy is nothing?' "

2. Fat as four bags of flax.
•   Ted Swidzinski of Kamsack, Saskatchewan, heard this description of a hefty farm lady from a district farmer and neighbour, William Doodchenko.

3. A good workman always builds a shed over his best tool.
• This is a portly gentleman's reply when criticized for his beer belly.

4. She's a tub of shit. In fact, when she takes a dump, four men gotta roll her up to a cement-mixer and wedge her in.

5. He's so fat he sat on the rainbow and Skittles popped out.

6. He's so fat when he swims in the ocean whales sing "We are family."

7. He's such a lard-ass he irons his pants in the driveway with an asphalt roller.
   Dawn Rusnak, Delhi, Ontario

8. So fat we had to sit him in a corner and feed him with a slingshot.
   Len Ross, North Bay, Ontario

9. Everything moves but his bowels.
• Everything jiggles when he walks.

10. When she bends over, her heart stops.

96. FEAR

1. That's a real turd-curdler.
• Very scary!

Bill Turner, Brandon, Manitoba

2. The wrinkles dropped right out of my bag.
• You were very frightened and you produced one
of the typical physiological signs of male fear. The
cremaster muscle, suspended under the testicles,
retracts and the scrotum is drawn up close to the
body. This cremasteric reflex happens when men are
very cold, during the fight-or-flight response to shock,
fear or severe stress, and just prior to orgasm. It acts
to keep the testes warm, to protect them from injury,
and to increase the propulsive force of seminal
emission by decreasing the distance the ejaculate must
travel during orgasm. The reflex can also be produced
by stroking the inside part of a man's thigh in a
downward direction. The normal response in males is
a contraction of the cremasteric muscle that pulls up
the scrotum and testis on the side stroked. However
the saying is not totally correct. Although they may
seem to, the wrinkles, the muscular corrugations of
the scrotal sack, do not in fact disappear during
cremasteric contraction.

Perhaps I can toss in here an old, hoary
medical-school joke? A man goes to a doctor and

presents with a large abnormal mass in his throat. The patient tells the doctor it took him weeks to get up the courage to enter the doctor's office because he is terrified of medicine and of doctors in particular, due to an unfortunate childhood incident. The doctor palpates the mass in his throat, determines its motility, assures himself that it is not merely something swallowed, a bolus of compacted food lodged in the throat. Nor is it to the physician's satisfaction a goitre. The patient's thyroid is just dandy. Finally, after exhausting his diagnostic prowess, the doctor sighs and prepares to take a biopsy, a tissue sample of the throat lump. He sends it off to the pathology lab to determine precisely what kinds of cells comprise this mysterious lump. A few days later the quaking patient sits before him in the consulting room. "Mr. Jones, you **were** frightened to come to my consulting room. That lump is the result of the most powerful cremasteric reflex known to medical literature!"

Okay, it's not *that* funny a joke. But it helps medical students remember the cremaster muscle.

97. FERTILITY

1. Your mother was so fertile I could spit on her and she'd get pregnant.

98.   FICKLE FATE

1. Chickens one day, feathers the next.
- Some days you win; some days you don't.

   Alice Morin, Saskatchewan

99.   FLATULENCE

1. Who stepped on the duck?

2. Wherever you go
Let the wind go free,
For keeping my wind,
Was the death of me.
- This advice was spotted carved on an Irish
gravestone by Brendan J. O'Byrne of Regina.

3. Better out than your eye, and the hole is half as
sore.
- This is said after a particularly loud fart. A
gouged eye socket hurts much more than one's anus
presumably tattered after a mighty breaking of wind.

   Steve McCabe, Oakville, Ontario

4. A fart's the crookedest thing in the world; it's
aimed at your heels and hits your nose.

5. The pitter-patter of soft steppers.
This describes a faint volley of almost inaudible but

genuine farts. In my public school days in
Dunnville, the effect was also known as doing
"a far-off motorboat."

Len Ross, North Bay, Ontario

6. Oh, go wipe your ass and call it a shit.
• This is said after a loud fart.

100. FOOD

1. A hot dog feeds the hand that bites it.

Cogie Drose, Chipman, New Brunswick

2. Don't be hungry like at home.
• Dawn Rusnak of Delhi, Ontario, writes: "This is
what my grandpa, Big Mike, used to say to company
to encourage them to eat more. He came to Canada
from Czechoslovakia in the 1940s." Whether the
saying harks back to tough times in the old country
or whether it means that guests usually have scanty
meals at their home is not clear.

3. Kill-me-quicks.
• A reader who wishes to remain anonymous writes,
"I saw you on TV today with Vickie Gabereau and was
reminded of all the funny sayings my grandma used.
One thing that she and all the other ladies of the
Huntsville Ontario Ladies Aid used to say got me into

trouble in school. They were always baking for afternoon teas and they called their cookies and cakes 'kill-me-quicks.' The ladies said the words very quickly. As a child I thought that was the word for any kind of baked goodie. One day in Grade One—kindergarten did not exist yet—I offered my teacher a kill-me-quick and had no idea why she was so angry and made me stand in the corner. It did serve to make me more accepting of the children in my future classes when later I became a teacher."

4. Bad enough to give a gopher heartburn.
• Quoted by W.O. Mitchell in one of his early stories, possibly *Jake & the Kid*, this is a Canadian Prairie original.

5. Q: What's for dinner?
   A: Horseshit and shavings.
• "My mom, Fern Boomhower, used this saying when we kids would pester her about what was for dinner," writes Darren Boomhower of Calgary.

6. Child: What's for dessert?
   Unsympathetic adult at table: Desert the table!
   Lachlan Fulton, Saint John, New Brunswick

7. Duck under the table and a farting clapper.
• Dick Heggs of the Okanagan Valley in British

Columbia writes, "When I asked my mother what was for dinner, this was a frequent reply."

8. She made this with her own two little hooves.
• This sarcastic put-down about bad food is uttered by someone who will never have to worry again about being served by the person to whom the bovine insult was addressed.

101. FOOLISHNESS
1. He puts the *dick* into *ridiculous*.
   Len Ross, North Bay, Ontario

102. FOREIGN-LANGUAGE SAYINGS
Some of these are heard in Canada and are used by Canadians who have a second language. So I've sprinkled a few on this word-feast to add spice and variety.

1. *Die Julisonne arbeitet für zwei.*
• The July sun does the work of two, according to this German saying.

2. *Hawawa ka he'e nalu haki ka papa.*
• 'When the surf rider is unskilled, the board is broken.' In the lovely Polynesian consonant–vowel

BILL CASSELMAN

rhythm of this Hawaiian proverb there is also a sexual connotation: when the man is unskilled, the woman is dissatisfied.

See also the category Elevators *for more foreign sayings.*

103. FRIGIDITY
1. She's an ice cube with a hole in it.

104. FUSSY EATERS
1. Fellow'd eat a lot of that afore he'd chew a stone.
• In days of yore, a rural mom might have said this to a child picking at his food.

105. GAIT
1. He walks like a ruptured duck.

106. GALL
1. Got a nerve on her like a toothache.
   Len Ross, North Bay, Ontario

107. GAY INSULTS

1. He can do more tricks on six inches of stiff dick than a monkey can do on a twenty-foot rope.

2. I hope you don't mind sitting on the floor? We can't afford to lose another sofa.
- This suggests that the gay guest has so distended an anus from being sodomized that on his last visit the sofa disappeared up his ass.

3. Did you hear about the gay burglar? He couldn't blow the safe, so he went down on the elevator.

4. You're alone for the weekend? I know you can't use a carrot anymore. It'd get lost. How about a pumpkin?
- Like a lot of queenly humour, this implies a stretched anus from inserting various objects into it.

5. You've taken it up the Hershey highway for years and you're still poor. Ever think about putting a tollbooth on your ass?

6. Where do you sleep when they lock the park?
- This implies wanton public sex and poverty so dire the person has no home.

7. He's as queer as a football bat.
- This saying is mildly homophobic.

8. Queer? He's taken it up the rear so deep his ears lit up.

9. He doesn't know Dorothy.
• This outmoded gay code sentence means: he's straight as opposed to homosexual. The 1940s expression refers to every gay man's supposedly delirious affection for Judy Garland movies, particularly the girl she plays in *The Wizard of Oz*.

108. GOOD LUCK
1. Even a blind hog will find an acorn once in a while.

109. GRACE AT TABLE
1. Good bread, good meat; Good God, let's eat!
   Christopher Melsted, Banff, Alberta

110. GREETINGS
1. How's your dink for wrinkles?

2. How's your bird?
In this very informal greeting, bird refers to either sex's genitalia.
   Len Ross, North Bay, Ontario

111. GUILT

1. I was holding the parcel when the wrap fell off.
• Caught in the act, eh?

112. HAIR

1. Her hairdo looked like a hen's arse in a windstorm.

Lloyd Candow, Pasadena, Newfoundland

2. Can't get the will-knots out—even with two combs.
• The pun concerns little balls of adhesive crud stuck in hair that just **will not** come out.

Len Ross, North Bay, Ontario

113. HAPPINESS

1. Too much sunshine makes a desert.

2. Smiling like a girl pig peeing.

114. HATRED

1. I wouldn't cross the street to piss on him if he were on fire or even just starting to smoulder.

115. HEALTH

1. Beef to the heels.

• Occasionally Canadian ears hear an Irish version of this expression: "beef to the heels from Mullingar." Mullingar (population about 12,500) is the county town of Westmeath in Leinster. A popular resort, Mullingar is on the N4, which is the main road west from Dublin. Greyhound racing happens nearby, as does trout fishing on the many lakes around Mullingar and there's a fine beach at Lilliput on nearby Lough Ennell. Mullingar is a rich cattle-producing area, so the well-fed girls that came to the City were described with this admiring phrase. No scrawny, anorexic city women for those bhoyos! Other variants are "beef to the hoof" and "beef to the ankles."

Brendan J. O'Byrne, Regina, Saskatchewan

2. Q: How's Fred doing these days?

A: They've buried people who look better than Fred.

• This retort was borrowed into Toronto English directly from Yiddish. One transliterated version of the Yiddish saying is *shainera menchen haut Fred gelicht in drert*, literally 'better-looking guys than Fred lie in the earth.'

116. HEARING

1. There's not a thing wrong with her hearing; she can hear milk curdle.
• A son describes his ninety-year-old mother's hearing.

G. Wright, Saskatoon, Saskatchewan

117. HEFT

1. She's two axe handles across the beam.
• She's a stocky gal with broad hips.

Gloria Onstad, Saskatchewan

2. Last time I saw an arse that wide it was pulling a wagon.

Len Ross, North Bay, Ontario

118. HESITATION

1. If *ifs* and *ands* were pots and pans,
   There'd be no work for tinkers' hands.
• A tinker was a wandering handyman who repaired household utensils. His implements, hung from the sideboards, tinkled as his wagon or cart travelled the bumpy country roads of yore. Because rumour said that tinkers swore and cursed frequently, their cussing was without value—hence the saying "not worth a tinker's damn."

119. HOME

1. Never shit in your own pew.
• Don't do something stupid close to home.

  Len Ross, North Bay, Ontario

2. Seen their place? Early Sally Ann.
• This refers to a home-decorating job using furniture bought cheap at a Salvation Army thrift shop.

3. Born on a raft.
• This is said of a person who carelessly leaves doors and windows open.

120. HOUSEKEEPING

1. Shut the door. It's not an asshole that closes by itself.
• This tart rebuke was heard in the vicinity of Rockglen, Saskatchewan.

121. HUMILITY

1. *On est venu au monde pour un petit pain.*
• Carmen P. Joynt of Nanaimo emails, "My mother often used this phrase, which I disliked immensely. It means 'we were born for a small loaf of bread' and implies that we were not born to become very important people."

122. HUNGER

1. I'm so hungry I could eat a scabby-headed bairn.
- Bairn is Scottish dialect for 'small child.'

2. I could eat a farmer's arse through a hedge.
   Martin Cristopher, Springside, Saskatchewan

123. HYPERACTIVITY

1. She runs the roads night and day.
- Some are always on the go.
   Len Ross, North Bay, Ontario

124. IGNORANCE

1. You don't know shit from dirty putty.

125. ILLNESS

1. Cancer, schmancer—as long as you're healthy.
- A *bissel* of Yiddish irony underlies this saying.

2. Is he sick? Hell, he's overdue for reincarnation.

126. IMPATIENCE

1. Don't be such a kipper waitress.
- This is the personal coinage of Harold Millie of
Pilot Butte, Saskatchewan, who, while sojourning in

England, encountered impatient waitresses who remove plates from restaurant tables before diners have finished eating the food. Kipper is slang for 'an English person,' based on the fact that kipper is also the salted, dried herring served during some English breakfasts.

127. INCOMPETENCE

1. He couldn't organize a piece of ass in a whorehouse.

2. He couldn't find his arse with both hands and a flashlight.

Bill Turner, Brandon, Manitoba

128. INDEPENDENCE

1. Deaf, blind, drunk—and still wants to cross the street on his own.

Ted Brown, North Vancouver, British Columbia

129. INDIFFERENCE

1. If I gave a shit, you'd be the first one I'd give it to.

Len Ross, North Bay, Ontario

130. INEXPRESSIVENESS
1. She didn't say yes, no, kiss my arse, wind my watch, or meet me out behind the barn.
• Her lack of acknowledgment proved annoying.

Len Ross, North Bay, Ontario

131. INFORMATION
1. On a need-to-know basis, I don't.

132. INSEPARABILITY
1. They go everywhere hanging onto each other's belts.

Len Ross, North Bay, Ontario

133. INSIGNIFICANCE
1. I took my pants off for that?
• The business endeavour or sexual encounter did not prove worthwhile.

134. INTELLIGENCE
1. Bright as a new moon on a cloudy night.

135. IN THE PAST

1. Back when you were a bump in your father's blue jeans.

136. IN THE WAY

1. You'd make a better door than a window.

   Len Ross, North Bay, Ontario

2. You're like a goddamn obstacle course.

137. IRRELEVANCE

1. That doesn't mean shit to a tree.

   Doug Powers, Manitowaning, Ontario

138. KEEPING BUSY

1. Younger woman to a much older woman: How **do** you put in the time, dear?
Older Woman: Oh, it takes all my time just to get the crumbs out of my kitchen drawers.

   Julia Dickhout, Dunnville, Ontario

139. KNOCKED OUT COLD

1. Tits up and smiling at the moon.

   Len Ross, North Bay, Ontario

140. KNOWING SOMEONE WELL

1. *Je te connais comme si je t'avais tricoté.*
• I know you as if I had knitted you. A mother might say this to an older child who is trying to deceive the mother.

Carmen P. Joynt, Nanaimo, British Columbia

141. KNOW-IT-ALLS

1. Right. And I bet you can sit on ice cream and tell what flavour it is too?
• That would be one smart ass!

Brendan J. O'Byrne, Regina, Saskatchewan

2. You've been everywhere, haven't you, skipper?
• This is a rebuke to a traveller–braggart.

Doug Powers, Manitowaning, Ontario

142. LAUGHTER

1. I laughed so hard a tear ran down my leg.

Ted Brown, North Vancouver, British Columbia

143. LAZINESS

1. He's so lazy his weight's no good on a pry.
• This might arise when prying up something large with, say, two men pushing down on a large crowbar.

Lachlan Fulton, Saint John, New Brunswick

2. Get your finger out of your bum and your mind out of neutral.
• Petty Officers in the Royal Canadian Navy issued this curt order to chastise idle or absent-minded sailors.

3. Some people are like prunes. You know they're going to work. You just don't know when.

4. They call him "Blister." He shows up after the work is all done.

5. He thinks Manual Labour is a Spanish dancer.

144. LEARN BY READING
1. The brain can only absorb what the ass can endure.
   Brendan J. O'Byrne, Regina, Saskatchewan

145. LETTER WRITING
1. Paper has never refused ink.
• One meaning is plaintive: write once in a while.
   Brendan J. O'Byrne, Regina, Saskatchewan

146. LIARS
1. You can't trust him any farther than you can see up a moose's asshole in a snowstorm.

2. She's farting through her mouth.

> Bill Turner, Brandon, Manitoba

3. Tell that to a dead horse and he'll kick your brains out.
- It's a reply when you have heard what you know is an outright lie.

> Lloyd Candow, Pasadena, Newfoundland

4. He is ten pounds of shit in a five-pound bag, with a rope tied tight around the middle.

147. LIVING SPACE
1. It's so small you can't swing a cat around in it.
- Michael Moore of Vancouver writes, "My father uses it frequently when describing cramped quarters like tiny apartments."

148. LOOSE WOMEN
1. Q: How long has Tiffany been like that?
   A: She was a whore as a fetus.
- This is an adaptation of a Yiddish expression, *Sie haut gevain a courva schon in de momma's bouch,* literally 'she was a whore already in her mother's tummy.' Bouch is 'stomach,' a euphemism for womb.

149. LOUDNESS

1. That guitar amp will part your hair at fifteen paces.

150. LOYALTY

1. That dog sticks to her like shit sticks to fur.

Mary Massey, Penetanguishene, Ontario

151. LUDDITE FOREVER

1. He's still sending messages with his secret decoder ring from Captain Midnight.

152. MACHISMO

1. Who is the handsomest man here and why am I?

Rex Summersides

2. He's a slap hunky.
• This is heard in North Winnipeg, said of a male who tries too hard, a poser, a wannabe stud.

Matthew Pesclovitch, Winnipeg, Manitoba

3. The dick-waggers are on the way.
• This is corporate jargon. It signifies that the "suits" are here, that is, swaggering high-ranking executives have entered the building.

4. He had a cock long as a four-dollar skipping rope.

5. He had a hard-on that a bulldog couldn't chew.
   Len Ross, North Bay, Ontario

6. Ready? Hey, girl, if the wind changes direction,
I get a hard-on.

153. MARRIAGE
Yes, some of these wheezers are so old that the late
Henny Youngman (1906-1998) used them in his
pioneering stand-up routines in which he spritzed
one-liners at the audience almost faster than they could
hear them.

1. What's all the fuss about same-sex marriage? I've
been married for years, and I keep having the same
sex.

2. My wife will buy anything marked down. Last year
at The Bay she bought an escalator.

3. A fortune teller told her that her husband would
die by poisoning, and she asked, "Will I be acquitted?"

4. His wife asked to be seen in something long and
flowing—so he dropped her in the river.

5. Sure, married men live longer than single men, but married men are a lot more willing to die.

6. I got a new car for my wife. It was a great trade.

7. Cannibals won't eat divorced women. They're very bitter.

8. You never realize how short a month is until you pay alimony.

9. Are you a man or a mouse? Squeak up!

10. Marriage is like a bank account. You put it in, you take it out, you lose interest.

11. My wife and I were happy for twenty years, then we met.

12. I still miss my ex-wife. But my aim is getting better.

13. I take my wife everywhere, but she keeps finding her way back.

14. An early hanging can prevent a bad marriage.
• The supply of creepy potential bridegrooms ought

to be winnowed by fate and justice. This saying is at least four hundred years old. In act one of *Twelfth Night* written in 1601, Shakespeare quotes this old saw (1.v.19-20) "Many a good hanging prevents a bad marriage."

15. God made them and the devil matched them.
• Said of a bride and groom with little hope of a lasting union.

Lloyd Candow, Pasadena, Newfoundland

16. For every Jean there is a Jock.
• Scotland gave us this optimistic forecast of connubial pairing.

17. "This is something my husband said to me. I think it could be filed under 'good-natured banter.' He was pestering me about something. I said, 'I don't know why I put up with you.' He replied, 'Putting up with me is the best thing you have going for you.' "

Teresa Sinkowski, Waterford, Ontario

Yes, some of these are rhymes not sayings, but—know what?—enjoy them anyway!

18. Marry a mountain woman and you marry the mountain.

19. Marry in May and rue the day,
    Marry in Lent and you'll to repent,
    Marry in green, ashamed to be seen,
    Marry in blue and always be true,
    Marry in red, sure to be dead,
    Marry in yellow, ashamed of your fellow,
    Marry in white, marry all right,
    Marry in grey and live far away,
    Marry in black, sure to come back,
    Marry in brown and live out of town.

20. The Days for Marriage:
    Monday for health,
    Tuesday for wealth,
    Wednesday the best day of all.
    Thursday for losses,
    Friday for crosses,
    Saturday no day at all.

21. If you marry and the old fellow's cross,
    Lift the poker saying, "I'm the boss."

154. MASTURBATION

Here are a couple hundred synonyms used chiefly by Canadian males to refer to the act. Several readers have chided me for leaving out variants and well-known sayings in both previous volumes of Canadian Sayings.

So, for this one category, I decided to include nearly every pertinent saying that I have collected or been sent on the topic. The large number of phrases and expressions demonstrates how easily one could fill thick books with variants—if little or no editorial judgment was brought to bear on how much to include. Of course, I think some of these synonyms, euphemisms, and parallel phrases are very funny. That's the main reason they're here. Some phrases I omitted due to contemporary references that might date quickly, i.e. "dating Palm-ela Handerson."

Many religious references also seemed de trop, such as "Onan's Olympics" and "disobeying the Pope." So, does this list contain all English sayings about masturbation? No, not by a long shot.

1. Answer the bone-a-phone.
2. Assault on a friendly weapon.
3. Backstroke roulette.
4. Bait your hook.
5. Batting practice.
6. Bash the candle.
7. Beat off.
8. Beat the bait.
9. Beat the bishop.
10. Beat the dummy.
11. Beat the snake.
12. Beat the stick.

13. Beat your meat.
14. Be your own best friend.
15. Bleed the weed.
16. Blow your load.
17. Bludgeon the beefsteak.
18. Bop your bologna.
19. Box the Jesuit.
20. Bringing Mr. Weasel back from the dead.
21. Buff the banana.
22. Buff the woody.
23. Burp the worm.
24. Butter your corn.
25. Call down for more mayo.
26. Calling all cum.
27. Carry weight.
28. Cast off.
29. Change your oil.
30. Charm the cobra.
31. Choke Charlie until he throws up.
32. Choke the sheriff and wait for the posse to come.
33. Choke your chicken.
34. Civil war.
35. Clean out your rope.
36. Clean the pipes.
37. Clean your rifle.
38. Club Eddy.
39. Couch hockey for one.
40. Crack the fat.

41. Crank for cum.
42. Crank the shank.
43. Crank your case.
44. Crown the king.
45. Cuff the carrot.
46. Cuff the puppy.
47. Cum the scum.
48. Custer's last stand.
49. Date Miss Michigan.
50. Date Ma Palm and her five daughters.
51. Devil's handshake.
52. Diddle your piddle.
53. Dishonourable discharge.
54. Disseminate.
55. Doddle your whacker.
56. Doodle your noodle.
57. Download from your own website.
58. Drain the dragon.
59. Drain the monster.
60. Drain the vein.
61. Drop a line.
62. Drop stomach pancakes.
63. Evict the testicular squatters.
64. Fist-fuck fer fun.
65. Fist your mister.
66. Five against one.
67. Five-finger knuckle shuffle.
68. Five-knuckle Olympics.

69. Flog your dong.

70. Flog your log.

71. Flute solo.

72. Flying a kite.

73. Fondle the fig.

74. Free the Willies.

75. Frig the love muscle.

76. Gallop the antelope.

77. Gallop the maggot.

78. Get in touch with your manhood.

79. Get in touch with yourself.

80. Get your caps peeled.

81. Give it a tug.

82. Give the John Hancock.

83. Grease the pipe.

84. Grease your handle.

85. Hack the hog.

86. Ham shank.

87. Hand job.

88. Hands-on training.

89. Hand-to-gland combat.

90. Hand work.

91. Have a roy.

92. Have it off.

93. Have one off the wrist.

94. Hitchhike under the big top.

95. Hitch to heaven.

96. Hit the ham.

97. Hold all the cards.

98. Hold a staff meeting.

99. Hold your sausage hostage.

100. Hone your bone.

101. Hump air.

102. Hump your fist.

103. Hump your hose.

104. Iron some wrinkles.

105. Jack.

106. Jackin' the beanstalk.

107. Jack off.

• This originates as a slang form of the verb *ejaculate*.

108. Jack the hammer.

109. Jag off.

110. J. Arthur Rank.

• This perhaps originates as Cockney rhyming slang in which the name of a once familiar British film studio and distributor is substituted for some locution such as 'jag your crank.'

111. Jazz yourself.

112. Jelly roll.

113. Jenny McCarthy jaunt.

114. Jerkin' the gherkin.

115. Jerk off.

116. Jerk the johnson.

117. Jiggle your jewellery.

118. Jimmy your joey.

119. Kill the beast.

120. Knock the top off the column.
121. Knuckle-shuffle your duffel and bag.
122. Land the pink fish.
123. Launch the hand shuttle.
124. Launch the tadpoles.
125. Make nut butter.
126. Make the bald guy puke.
127. Make yogurt.
128. Make your mule mope.
129. Mangle the midget.
130. Manipulate the mango.
131. Manual override.
132. Masonic secret self-shake.
133. Massage the old love muscle.
134. Massage your purple-headed warrior.
135. Measure for a new condom.
136. Milk the bull.
137. Milk the lizard.
138. Milk the monkey.
139. Milky Waying.
140. Mould hot plastic.
141. Oil the glove.
142. Oil the pogo stick.
143. One-handed clapping.
144. One-man tug-of-war.
145. Open the one-man show.
146. Pack your palm.
147. Paddle the pickle.

148. Paint the pickle.
149. Paste your fingers.
150. Pat the Robertson.
151. Peel a chili.
152. Peel the banana.
153. Peel the carrot.
154. Pet the dog.
155. Play a solo on the meat whistle.
156. Play pocket pinball.
157. Play pocket pool.
158. Play the organ.
159. Play the pisser.
160. Play the piss pipe.
161. Play the skin flute.
162. Play the stand-up organ.
163. Play with Dick.
164. Play with Susie Palmer and her five friends.
165. Play with the snake.
166. Play with your noodle.
167. Play with yourself.
168. Play your instrument.
169. Polish the rocket.
170. Polish the sword.
171. Polish your bayonet.
172. Polish your helmet.
173. Polish your piece.
174. Pop the porpoise.
175. Pound 'er like a flounder.

176. Pound off.
177. Pound your pud.
178. Practise one-upmanship.
179. Pull a one-liner.
180. Pull your wire.
181. Punchin' the munchkin.
182. Punch the clown.
183. Punishing the bishop.
184. Rope the longhorn.
185. Round up the tadpoles.
186. Rub the unicorn's horn.
187. Shake hands with a member of the House.
188. Shoot putty at the moon.
189. Slap-box the one-eyed champ.
190. Slap Pappy.
191. Slap the salami.
192. Spread the mayo.
193. Spunk the monk.
194. Squeeze the cream from the Twinkie.
195. Take a shake break.
196. Tease the python.
197. Tenderize your tube-steak.
198. Tug the tapioca tube.
199. Unwrap the pepperoni.
200. Walk Willie, the one-eyed wonder-worm.
201. Wank your crank.
202. Warm up the altar boy's dinner.
203. Wind the jack-in-the-box.

204. Wrestle the eel.
205. Yank Hank.
206. Zap your chap.
207. Zonk your bronc.

155. MATURITY

1. He's big enough to burn diesel.

    Andy Fusick, Saskatoon, Saskatchewan

156. MEANNESS

1. He broke into the CNIB to flatten out all the Braille.

• The Canadian National Institute for the Blind was no doubt amused at the practical joke. This saying is a pretty apt sample of the true mentality of practical jokers. They are, for the most part, not very bright, nasty, bullying morons.

2. She wouldn't knit an ass for a cat.

3. He would throw a drowning man both ends of the rope just to see the look on his face.

157. MEMORY

1. I used to have a photographic memory, but lately I forget to put the film in.

Kevin Yaromich, Bismarck, Ontario

158. MEN

1. Men are just little boys in long pants.

Lachlan Fulton, Saint John, New Brunswick

159. MENSTRUATION

1. There are Communists in the summerhouse.

2. Aunt Rose is visiting from Potsdam.
• Both these creative Norwegian euphemisms for menstruation, translated and used in English in Ontario and Manitoba, were sent to me by a woman in Northern Ontario who remembers, as a little girl, hearing them from her mother. The Communists in the summerhouse may be a reference to the Red Army, for the same description of the Russian Army appears in Norwegian.

3. *Tante Rosa kommt aus Deutschland.*
• 'Aunt Rose is coming from Germany.' This is a common German euphemism once used by some German-speaking women in Canada. It's a variant of the expression used in Germany: *Tante Rosa kommt aus Amerika.*

4. Aunt Flo is visiting this week.

5. The Russians are attacking.

6. I used to be a seamstress but I had to quit.
Couldn't mend straight.
• This is a schoolboy's giggle after he discovers a few facts of life.

7. The snowbanks are spotted.

8. All is not quiet on the waterfront.

9. The domestic affliction is upon us.

10. The curse of Eve has fallen.

11. She's entertaining the general.

12. The red flag is up on the canal.

13. Red Emma has come to tea.

14. It's high tide in the narrows.

15. The gate is locked and the key is lost for now.

16. There are red sails in the sunset.

17. Like Lady Godiva, she's riding the white horse.

18. The woman's home companion has arrived.

19. Little Red got through the small door.

20. Mommy's got a red tummy-ache.

160. MESSINESS

1. Hell, west and crooked.
•   Devon Brown has heard this phrase used up and down the Annapolis Valley in Nova Scotia. It describes anything scattered about. A mom might chastise her son thus: "Clean up your room! You've got toys strung out Hell, west and crooked."

2. I'm going to bang nails into the floor so you'll have somewhere to hang your clothes.
•   This is an Edmonton mother telling her son to clean up his room.

3. What we got here is the afterbirth of a Martian grudge-fuck.

Len Ross, North Bay, Ontario

4. He's one drool bib short of neat and tidy.

161. MIND YOUR OWN BUSINESS
1. Go fruit on your own loom.

> Phoenix Wisebone, Vancouver, British Columbia

162. MISTAKES
1. If mistakes were haystacks, we'd all keep a cow.
• Lachlan Fulton of Saint John reports this saying of a local character from the little lumbertown of Chipman, New Brunswick. A gent named Cogie Drose ran a hotdog cart on Saturdays. Chipman townsfolk going to the movie theatre on Saturday night would buy a hotdog and hear Cogie's latest sayings. Naturally many of his expressions concerned frankfurters. Cogie always said, "A hotdog feeds the hand that bites it."

163. MODERATION
1. Don't dig up more snakes than you can kill.

164. MOVEMENT
1. Up and down faster than Mary's pants at a picnic.

165. MOVIE REVIEW
1. I've seen better film on my teeth.

> Phoenix Wisebone, Vancouver, British Columbia

166. NAÏVETÉ

1. You think I came down with the last rain?

Len Ross, North Bay, Ontario

167. NASTINESS

1. Mean as cat piss.
• This may refer to a rank odour, to someone very cheap, or to a curmudgeon.

Len Ross, North Bay, Ontario

168. NO IS THE ANSWER

1. Do cows shit cupcakes?

2. I would rather have all my teeth removed by a one-armed ass-scratcher.
• One correspondent wrote me that this was "an airline expression of Scottish origin via South Africa, India and the Middle East." Quite the travelled phrase!

169. NOISE

1. Noisier than Orville Redenbacher's barn burning.

Bill Turner, Brandon, Manitoba

2. Noisy as two skeletons dancing on a tin roof.

170. NOSE-PICKING
1. Adult to a child picking his or her nose: You'll need a safety helmet.
Child: Why?
Adult: You're mining for green nuggets.
   Derek J. Carr, White Rock, British Columbia

171. NOTHING NEW UNDER THE SUN
1. Same whore; new dress.

172. NUISANCE
1. He's a real balls' ache.
• It's an originally Australian expression meaning he's a pain in the ass.

173. OBJECT OF NOTE
1. She's quite the rig.

174. OBSTACLE
1. It's the longest tooth in the poll.
• Poll means head, as in poll tax or head tax. Mattie Carpenter writes, "I recently heard a Canadian say this

in a formal military briefing to mean an obstruction to good order or flow." It's a variant of "the long pole in the tent," that is, the one that is going to cause trouble.

175. OBVIOUSNESS
1. Wearing white socks in a coal mine.
- They would stick out like a sore thumb.
  Len Ross, North Bay, Ontario

176. ODDNESS
1. Queerer than a cat fart.

177. OLD AGE
1. Older than the back of God's head.
  Glenn Froh of Lethbridge, Alberta; Guelph, Ontario, and Weyburn, Saskatchewan

2. I'm so old I sold tickets to the Last Supper.
  Ken Ruller, Calgary, Alberta

3. He held the camels for the three Wise Men.
  Len Ross, North Bay, Ontario

4. Rebuke to youthful co-workers by a woman of a certain age: I have shoes older than you!

Pat Doer, Winnipeg, Manitoba

5. Grey as a badger.
• "My husband's grandmother used this saying to refer to people with extensive grey hair," writes Shirley Miller of Regina. "Gram was born in Scotland and lived the majority of her life in Saskatchewan."

178. OPINIONS

1. Opinions are like assholes: everyone has one.

Steve McCabe, Kenilworth, Ontario

2. If I wanted to hear from an asshole, I would've farted.
• Keep your opinion to yourself.

Bob Richardson, West Garafraxa Township, Wellington County, Ontario

179. ORDERS

1. Sorry, discussion has ended. I must now invoke the JFDI principle.
• Just Fucking Do It.

180. OVERCHARGING

1. I don't mind feeding you but I don't want you sitting at my table.

• "This was a nasty little insult from a farmer customer who felt he was overcharged because there was a new vehicle sitting in front of my father's house," writes Jim Rudd of The Pas, Manitoba.

181. PATHOS

1. You look like a little frozen turd in a matchbox.

182. PAYING ATTENTION

1. Take the cotton batten out of your ears and put it in your mouth.

• In other words, listen and then shut up.

Ted Brown, North Vancouver, British Columbia

183. PERSISTENCE

1. Sticks like shit to a wool army blanket.

• Nick Smith of Manitoba writes, "My grandfather from the Renfrew area of the Ottawa Valley was fond of this saying."

184. PICKING & CHOOSING
1. A dog that shits fast don't shit long.
- In matters canine or human, one can't have it both ways.

185. PIETY AS SICKNESS
1. She's so devout that she's looking forward to death.

186. POLICE
1. The Brandon City Police couldn't track an elephant with a bloody nose through a six-foot snowdrift; but open a can of beer on the other side of town and they'll be on you in a second.
- Two elderly gentlemen in a Manitoba mall complain about the city police.

2. Off in the Queen's taxi.
- That is, in a cop car. Brent Wolters writes, "I was a cab driver for a number of years on Vancouver Island, and we had this phrase about cops who would arrest a customer in our cabs and haul them off to jail or Juvy Hall. A police car was the Queen's taxi, because they would pick you up anywhere, but only drop you off in one place. The cabbie of course usually lost his fare if a miscreant was nabbed in the taxi itself." Juvy Hall or juvy is any place of detention for juvenile offenders.

187. POLITICAL POSITION

1. Slightly to the right of Attila the Hun.

   Jim Maunder, Newfoundland

188. POMPOSITY

1. He's undergone a religious conversion; he no longer believes he's God.

2. She has found a new humility. Her latest book is *Famous People Who Have Met Me.*

189. POOR LAND & THIN SOIL

1. This land is so poor, a jackrabbit would have to pack a box lunch to cross it.

   Christopher Melsted, Banff, Alberta

190. POOR VISION

1. Blind as a boiled cod.

   Len Ross, North Bay, Ontario

191. POUTING

1. She had a lower lip on her like a school doorstep.

2. How about a ride on your lower lip?

3. She had a mug like a wet winter.
• All three sayings from my star contributor, Mr. Ross, mock someone who pouts.

Len Ross, North Bay, Ontario

192. POVERTY

1. We were so poor we couldn't buy a hummingbird a vest.

2. We were so poor we didn't have a pot to piss in or a window to throw it out of.

Bob Richardson, West Garafraxa Township, Wellington County, Ontario

3. Nothing to eat but bread and scrape.
• Phoenix Wisebone of Vancouver heard this around Middlesex County in the 1960s said by residents recently arrived from England. Scrape is drippings from the bottom of a roasting pan.

4. I'm so broke I couldn't afford a down payment on a penny match.

5. We were so poor I had to wear a hat to look out the window.

Len Ross, North Bay, Ontario

6. Too poor to paint, too proud to whitewash.

193. PREJUDICE

1. He was treated like a red-headed stepchild.

Len Ross, North Bay, Ontario

194. PRETENDING

1. You can put your boots in the oven, but it doesn't make them biscuits.

195. PRIORITY

1. We'll do that after we've dealt with the flying pigs.
• Hopeless or impossible ventures must wait until problems of a more realistic nature have been solved.

Jack Marsh, Barrow-in-Furness, Cumbria, UK

196. PROBLEMS

1. I see the fuck-up fairy has paid another visit.
• A recurring problem has resurfaced.

2. We gotta get rid of that buggerette.
• A small but recurring technical problem needs fixing.

3. Just like the constipated mathematician, I worked it out with a pencil.

4. Like a swallowed quarter, this too shall pass.
• You will survive most hardships or difficulties, however difficult to swallow.

Dave Harris, Petawawa, Ontario

197. PRODUCING
1. He couldn't produce a hard-on in a whorehouse with a credit card.

2. He couldn't produce a wet fart at a beer-drinking contest.

198. PROSPERITY
1. He's riding a gravy train with biscuit wheels.

199. QUICKNESS
1. He can blow out the lamp and be in bed before it gets dark.

2. Slicker than snot on a glass eye.

3. He's running like a man with a paper ass going through a forest fire.

200. QUIET

1. Quiet as an ant pissing on a cotton ball.
• Or even more noiseless: quiet as an ant thinking about pissing on a cotton ball.

> Bill Turner, Brandon, Manitoba

201. QUITTING TIME

1. Time to head home and see what the neighbours threw over the fence.

> Teresa Sinkowski, Waterford, Ontario

202. RACETRACK

1. That horse couldn't outrun a sock.
• Tim Gompf writes, "My brother used the saying today to describe one of our two-year-old geldings that he is planning to break to ride. Great looking young horse but has no speed at all. Probably it will make a kids' nag or a good trail-rider. I doubt he'll make it as a performance horse."

203. RCAF SAYINGS

1. Even the birds are walking.
• This assumes knowledge of an earlier expression: Only birds and fools would fly in this weather.

2. A fair-wear-and-tear machine.
• In other words, a razor blade. During World War II, Air Force stores would not replace a uniform if it was only getting a bit shabby, and wilful damage to a uniform was punishable. Fair wear and tear could be simulated by stroking a strategic area gently and repeatedly with a razor blade.

3. "She Kissed Me Between the Hangars Before I Went Off in the Air."
• Mildly obscene comic song titles were a pastime of Canadian Air Force personnel. This one was coined sometime during the Second World War, and has been winging its naughty way across tavern tables where airmen convene ever since. Something about breaking foam with fellow servicemen seems to inspire these larky song titles. Or is it just male lust?

204. READINESS
1. Just blacken my arse and call me a teakettle.
• I'm ready, willing, and able.
  Bill Turner, Brandon, Manitoba

205. READING
1. The brain can only absorb what the ass can endure.

- Most reading is indeed done while the reader is seated.

    Brendan J. O'Byrne, Regina, Saskatchewan

206. REALITY CHECK
1. If my aunt had balls, we would have called her uncle.

207. REJECTION
1. You are so off the island!
- This Canadian high-school slang arises from a moronic television program called *Survivor* in which a group of unpleasant people bivouacked in a deserted place or put ashore on some deservedly uninhabited island vote who among themselves should each week be cast forth from the group. It was an elimination contest—and I use the first noun in its biological sense too. The last person remaining on the island won prizes, presumably for being the most tribal of the assembled nincompoops.

    Ray Bélanger, St. John's, Newfoundland

208. RELIGION

1. There she was at Sunday Mass, biting the toenails off church statues.

• This expression from Ireland concerns the flamboyantly pious, those who must be seen being devout. It isn't enough to keep devotion modestly in one's heart. Oh no, one must rent a sound truck and drive through town broadcasting one's more creative novenas. The saying suggests that, deep within such showbizzy pieties, lurks religious hypocrisy. Showy devotees may sometimes be "street angels, house devils," that is, two-faced.

Brendan J. O'Byrne, Regina, Saskatchewan

209. RELUCTANCE

1. All iffy, like a virgin plucking a parson's pecker.
• Heard in Manitoba.

210. RESTAURANTS

1. Stay away from that ulcer gulch.

2. Ptomaine tent.

211. RESTAURANT SAYINGS TO ANNOY THE WAIT STAFF

1. Waitress: What'll you have?

    Customer: The sheep-herders breakfast.

    Waitress: Okay. I know I'm going to be sorry.
What's that?

    Customer: A glass of milk and a little bit of ewe.

212. RESTRAINT

1. Hold her down, Luke, she's headed for the barn.
•   This warning was heard if a piece of machinery being repaired was slipping out of the repairman's grasp or if a mighty blow with a big forge hammer was going to be required of a blacksmith handling an iron item hot from the forge. In origin, however, this expression stems from horse-drawn farm vehicles. If the hay-wagon horse suddenly bolted and put the load in danger, someone might shout this warning to the driver of the wagon. A variant appeared in volume two of *Canadian Sayings*: "Hold her, Newt, she's headed for the rhubarb!"

2. Hold on, Mama, the clutch is slipping.
•   "One of my current co-workers contributed this one and he says it means the same as the saying above but is originally from the lyrics to a Ukrainian song."

    Jim Rudd, The Pas, Manitoba

213. RUMOUR

1. That rumour spread faster than a fart through a cane-bottomed chair.

> Patti Moran, Ottawa, Ontario

214. SADNESS

1. I cried so much I didn't have to pee for a week.

2. He looks like the cheese fell off his cracker.

215. SALESMANSHIP

1. He couldn't sell sushi at a convention of Japanese muff-divers.

2. He could sell red baseball caps at a truck stop.

3. He could sell a ketchup Popsicle to a woman in white gloves.

4. He couldn't sell Chapstick at a cocksuckers' convention.

216. SARCASM

1. Sharper than a fishwife's tongue.

> Bill Turner, Brandon, Manitoba

217. SEARCHING IN VAIN

1. Like looking for tan lines on a nun.
• This describes what is difficult to find.

Len Ross, North Bay, Ontario

218. SELF-RELIANCE

1. Are you handcuffed and web-footed?
• Do it yourself.

219. SETBACKS

1. Remember, even a kick in the ass is one step forward.

Dawn Rusnak, Delhi, Ontario

220. SEX

1. Female hockey players are sexually aggressive; they always go too far. You know, icing the fuck.

2. I've seen bigger things in bad cheese.
• This began as a British schoolboy put-down of someone else's penis size. The implication is that the penis in question is smaller than a maggot squiggling through infested cheese. One correspondent also heard it after a fire at school from a school nurse who was applying medication to boys with burns. As they

undressed to receive inspection and salve, they were turning away bashfully so the nurse would not see their private parts, when the nurse uttered the line above.

3. That place is weenie-waggers' wonderland.
• This is a Canadian police term for a park or other locale frequented by men who expose themselves.

4. Q: Is she a virgin?
   A: Are you kidding? She spreads like peanut butter.

5. A male is born with a brain and a dick, but only enough blood to run one at a time.
• Comedian Robin Williams claims he wrote this jokey saying. So how does he explain its existence, a bit more politely phrased, in early twentieth-century printed texts, in both Russian and Yiddish. Come on, Robin, you heard it as a kid.

6. I could eat a yard of her shit kneeling on sandpaper.
• My, that lady is attractive.

7. She's so cold she spits ice cubes.

8. She had more ass than a toilet seat.
• One male brags to another male about a female conquest.

9. We got major-league Ripley here.
• Males ogling female breasts or a sexy figure refer to the character played by Sigourney Weaver in the *Alien* movies. To save her from the space monster, the male scriptwriters have Ripley always stripping to bikini briefs and easing herself provocatively into a metal pod.

Christopher Melsted, Banff, Alberta

10. She chased the minister round and round the church loft and finally caught him by the organ.

221. SEXIST INSULTS

1. Q: Why did God create the yeast infection?
A: So women too would know what it's like to live with an irritating cunt.

2. If he had a brain, he'd take it out and try to jerk it off.

3. Your sister is Little Bo P.E.E.P. (Perfectly Elegant Eatin' Pussy).

4. She does it so long she'll melt the fat off your bones.

5. She's hotter than a little red wagon.

6. She won't let anybody fuck her but her friends. Problem is, she hasn't got an enemy in the world.

7. The four-F school of courtship: Find 'em, feel 'em, fuck 'em, forget 'em.
•   This 1950s saying stayed current among macho males but lost favour during feminist times.

8. She's a ditch pig.
•   She's a slut who would fornicate at the side of the road at the drop of a one-dollar bill.

9. That skank is such a puck!
•   Such oinky rink talk echoes across our chauvinist land when urban hockey males are projecting their own self-loathing on easy women. This particular tag labels female hockey groupies. Skank is American Black slang for 'slut.' The reggae word *skanking* probably derives from the American term. When one dances the skank, one bends forward and raises the knees, and it suggests a sexual position—if you are a double-jointed lemur!

222. SEXUAL LOSER

1. The closest you get to pussy is gargling with a douche bag.
•   This male-to-male taunt bristles with loathing of

women. Picked up as jock talk from locker-room ribaldry, it was submitted from three universities in three different provinces. The war between the sexes has not seen its last battle.

223. SHIT HAPPENS
1. You can't polish a turd.

224. SHOWING OFF
1. Bet she wears white socks in a coal mine!

225. SHORTNESS
1. They built the sidewalk too close to Johnny's arse.

226. SIGNS
1. And no walking on the water!
•   This comic imperative appeared beneath a bulletin board in a church under a list of activities proscribed for Christian gentlefolk. It is the perfect squelch to officious and unnecessary bans of the kind pygmy bureaucrats are wont to issue every day on the hour.

Jack Marsh, Barrow-in-Furness, Cumbria, UK

227. SIMILARITY

1. You guys are two cheeks of the same ass.
- This snappy rebuke is heard frequently in Manitoba.

228. SIN

1. The Devil makes pots, but never lids.
- You can't hide your sins.

229. SLEEPING IN

1. What are you gonna do? Sleep 'til the sun shines up your arse?

Patrick Fusick, Saskatoon, Saskatchewan

230. SMALL AMOUNT

1. By a bee's dick.
- For example, he's clinging to sanity, but only by a bee's dick. Australian visitors and emigrants to Canada brought this expression from 'down under.'

2. Ten percent of bugger all is still bugger all.

Ted Brown, North Vancouver, British Columbia

3. Two-fifths of five-eights of fuck all.

231. SMALLNESS

1. Looks like a kitten on a Newfoundland dog.

2. It's about the width of a clergyman's mind.

Bill Turner, Brandon, Manitoba

232. SMOOTH TALKING

1. She can tell people to go to hell and they look forward to the trip.

Brendan J. O'Byrne, Regina, Saskatchewan

2. He's as smooth as piss on a plate.

233. SNOBBERY

1. Yeah, he's a real connoisseur—mostly sewer, with a touch of con.

Brendan J. O'Byrne, Regina, Saskatchewan

2. Put your nose down—before you trip over it.

Dawn Rusnak, Delhi, Ontario

3. Mrs. Letitia T. Clean Arse.
• It's a nickname for a stuck-up lady.

4. Her turds should be bronzed and sold as paperweights. Just ask her.

234. SPORTS

GOLF

1. That's ice cream on dog shit.
• Victor Slater of Toronto writes, "This golfing term refers to making an excellent shot late in an otherwise mediocre game."

FOOTBALL

1. Q: How do the Hamilton Tiger Cats keep their stadium grass trimmed?
     A: They let their cheerleaders graze.

HOCKEY

1. You couldn't put a puck in the ocean.

2. Put a helmet on these kids, and you get better conversation rubbing two sticks together.
• A hockey spectator is appalled at foul language heard during a peewee boys' game.

     Laurel Rice, heard in Dryden, Ontario

3. Bend over, Ref, so we can see your eyes!
• This is uttered to make clear one's displeasure at a hockey referee's ruling.

4. See you. Keep your stick on the ice.
• This is a farewell among players, like saying "drive safely."

     Hal B. and Don and Jeff O'Neil, Edmonton, Alberta

5. That goalie is a real noodle drainer.

6. That net-minder is made of Swiss cheese.

7. That bozo's a sieve.
• Too many pucks are getting past the goalie into the net.

   Christopher Melsted, Banff, Alberta

8. He couldn't find the puck or his pecker.
• Sticks are giving this hockey dude all kinds of woe.

9. He's a cherry picker.
• The hockey player hangs around the net waiting for a quick pass so he can slap the puck into the goal.

RODEOS

1. That horse couldn't run fast enough to scatter his own turds.
• A steer-wrestler said this about a horse that was too slow to be suitable for either roping off or steer wrestling.

2. That bull bucked through his asshole.
• This rodeo slang describes a really rank, hard-bucking bronc or bull.

3. He really roped the shit outta him.

• A rider makes a really fast run in the calf-roping event.

WRESTLING

1. It's a real ring-a-ding-dong dandy!
• Ed Whalen, the late Calgary commentator for Stampede Wrestling, used this catchphrase when a match heated up.

   Christopher Melsted, Banff, Alberta

235. SQUELCH FOR A PEST

1. Hey, if I want any shit out of you, I'll squeeze your head.
• Common in Windsor, Ontario, this excellent squelch ought to be more widely used.

   The Billingsley Family, McGregor, Ontario

236. STAG AT A PARTY

1. Go stag. It's more fun shopping when the basket is empty.
• This refers to a male going solo to a dance or party.

237. STATUS

1. I know him. He used to chew new bread for our ducklings.

• This implies he is a nobody, low on the scale of notability. From Alberta to our Maritimes some rural Canadians know this wonderful farm phrase. Baby ducklings choke on pulpy, gummy new bread. Therefore, it had to be broken up, if not chewed, when one was about to feed ducklings. Considered the lowliest job on the farm, bread breaking and chewing was the job of the hired farmhand with the least status or clout.

238. STINGINESS

1. Q: What's the difference between a Canadian and a canoe?

A: Sometimes a canoe tips.

2. Tighter than a vicar's sphincter.
• No doubt this assessment is that of a liberal Anglican.

3. They invented copper wire fighting over a penny.
   Brendan J. O'Byrne, Regina, Saskatchewan

4. He's tighter than floor wax.

5. He would take the sleep out of your eyes.

6. He's so cheap he takes off his glasses if he's not looking at anything.

Bill Turner, Brandon, Manitoba

7. He is so tight you couldn't pull a pin from his ass with a team of horses.

8. He is so cheap he wouldn't give you the steam off his piss.
• Many years ago, a man in Smithers, British Columbia, said this, complaining that he couldn't get the funding he needed for a project from a tight-fisted granting officer.

9. He's tighter than a fish's ass at fifty fathoms.

Shirley Miller, Regina, Saskatchewan

239. STORYTELLING
1. That's a real piss-cutter of a story.
• Medical query: does laughter cause sphincters to close, thus cutting off the flow of urine?

Lachlan Fulton, Saint John, New Brunswick

240. STRAIGHT AIM
1. He could shit through the eye of a needle at forty paces.

241. STRENGTH
1. Win a tug-of-war? That guy could pull the dark out of the night.

242. STUMBLING
1. On coming out of church, an elderly man slipped on the sidewalk and fell on his behind. After being teased by a crony that the sidewalks of Canada were too smart for him, he replied, "Smart as they are, I made them kiss my ass."

2. Have a nice trip. See you in the fall.

243. STUPIDITY
1. He's skating on the wrong surface of the ice.

2. She's taking a surfing vacation in Saskatchewan.

3. Just another example of true Canadian numb-nuttery.
• The deliciously silly noun *numb-nuttery* is an extension of the vocative insult "Hey! Numb nuts!" and seems to have originated in Ontario.

4. Centre shot!
• This insult is said to someone performing a stupid action.

The Billingsley Family, McGregor, Ontario

5. Stunned as a capelin.
• Gwen MacLennan of Stephenville, Newfoundland, writes, "This phrase was used by a friend of mine, Mr. Sheldon Hynes, when we were both attending the Nova Scotia Community College in Kentville, Nova Scotia. Sheldon is a native of Sop's Arm, Newfoundland, and is a great quoter of colourful turns of phrase." Capelin (traditional Newfoundland spelling is *caplin*) are small silvery saltwater fish, close relatives of freshwater smelt. A schooling species, capelin come ashore in vast, squiggling masses like smelt and are easily caught from a beach or dock. Thus they earn the reputation of being stupid. On the east coast of North America, capelin appear from Hudson Bay to Nova Scotia but are most abundant around Newfoundland and Labrador.

6. She's playing hockey with a warped puck.

7. She thinks intercourse is the break between classes.

Martin Cristopher, Springside, Saskatchewan

8. Dumb-ass? He had to be retrained after coffee break.

Brendan J. O'Byrne, Regina, Saskatchewan

9. The otoscope showed cobwebs.
• During his ear exam, the usual structures were absent, thus permitting a clear view within showing that there was no brain present.

10. If brains were gas, he wouldn't have enough to drive a gnat around the inside of a Cheerio.

11. If he had two clues, he'd send the one to look for the other.

12. He's a couple of feathers short of a chicken.

13. He's a few stars short of the Milky Way.

14. He couldn't find his ass with a funnel.

15. He doesn't know if his ass was bored, punched, or burnt out by lightning.
• This is a variant of expressions included in the previous two volumes of *Canadian Sayings*.

16. His puppies aren't barking in unison.

Denis Tremblay, Ontario

17. He wouldn't know if he'd been punched, power-drilled, or reamed out with a wood rasp.

Ted Brown, North Vancouver, British Columbia

18. Her book cover is great but the pages are blank.
• Said of a good-looking but dumb person.

19. Dumber than Joe Cunt's dog that swam across the river to get a drink of water.

20. A bright couple? She thinks Taco Bell is the Mexican phone company, whereas he knows it's the name of a Mexican prostitute who charges very modest fees.

21. If his I.Q. were any lower, we'd have to water him.

Len Ross, North Bay, Ontario

22. His mommy put him outside before the glue dried.

Len Ross, North Bay, Ontario

23. She lost her train of thought and the railroad was bust.

24. If all ten fingers were flashlights, he couldn't find his arse with both hands.

Len Ross, North Bay, Ontario

25. He ain't all coupled up.
• This is Prairie railroad slang.

26. It's not his fault; his parents dove into the shallow end of the gene pool.

Sarah Elvidge, Yarmouth, Nova Scotia

27. If brains were elastic, you wouldn't have enough to make a garter for a grasshopper.

28. If brains were dynamite, you couldn't blow dust off your hat.
• "I heard both sayings (27 and 28) in rural Saskatchewan," writes LaVerne Karras of Newmarket, Ontario.

29. Stunned as me arse.

Ray Bélanger, St. John's, Newfoundland

30. You could fall into a barrel of tits and come out sucking your thumb.

31. He's oatmeal north of the eyebrows.

32. Shoot low, sheriff, they're riding Shetlands.
• Everything you say is going over their heads. They are mental pygmies.

33. If brains were made of cotton, he wouldn't have enough to Kotex a mosquito.

34. She's not the brightest light in the harbour.

35. Dumb as a box of rocks.

    Jim Rudd, The Pas, Manitoba

36. If you eat acorns, you'll shit like a blue jay.
- Do what is unwise and suffer the consequence.

37. There is smoke from the chimney but no fire in the stove.
- The submitter of this old expression heard it said of a man who talked a lot but didn't say anything intelligent.

38. About as smart as a starving dog locked in a meat packer's.

39. Your wife has marital thrombosis. She's married to a clot.

40. You don't know crap from chocolate yogurt.

41. You don't know piles on a mule's arse from cherry pits.

42. Your brain isn't worth a piss-pot full of crabapples.

43. Some drink from the fountain of knowledge; you just gargle.

44. She spent twenty minutes staring at an orange-juice box because she saw the word *concentrate*.

45. He called the 7-Eleven to ask when they closed.

46. Plenty of myelin but not enough neurons.

47. Madame Zorra, the mind reader, charges him half price.

48. There's a kink in her Slinky.

49. He should have kept his helmet on when he took that Kawasaki Ninja 500R under the semi.

50. She wears a ponytail to cover up the valve stem.

51. She sat too long under the ozone hole.

52. His receiver is off the hook.

53. He thinks male zebras are the ones with the black stripes.

54. She's stumped by anything childproof.

55. Her source code is missing a few lines.

56. His mind's as empty as the sleeping-pill counter at a Niagara Falls motel.

57. A few guppies short of an aquarium.

58. A few beads short in her rosary.

59. A few beans short of chili.

60. A couple of slates short of a full roof.

244. SUCCESS

1. He's pissing in the tall weeds with the big dogs.
• He has found success at the office. A variant heard in the Ottawa Valley is "Head for the rhubarb; you're pissing with the big dogs now."

2. Now we're cooking! Let's turn up the gas.
• Things are working out, therefore let's go for it. Variant: We're cookin' on the front burner with the gas up high.

    Lee Wilson Wolfe, UK

245. SURPRISE

Some of the sayings here are also used to express vigorous approval.

1. Well, bugger me with a frozen porcupine.

2. Ream me out and pin me up to dry.
   Bill Turner, Brandon, Manitoba

3. Well, part my buttocks with a Christmas tree.

4. Well, that wipes the shit off the llama's ass.
   • It appears that Richard Robillard of Ontario created this zesty expression one night in a karaoke bar, after watching an old drunk mumble his way perilously through the tricky lyrics of a song and actually get to the final bars with the correct lyrics vocalized. It seemed miraculous that the inebriated singer did so.

5. Holy dyin' duck shit!
   • "My late father, Donald Boomhower, would say this, often when traffic in Belleville, Ontario, was heavy. It would be followed by 'Where are all these people coming from?' " writes Darren Boomhower of Calgary.

6. Well, slap a cedar shingle on my head and call me a shit house.

7. Now wouldn't that jar the heart of a wheelbarrow and the soul of a dishcloth!

Nellie Gardiner, Souris, Manitoba

8. Well, suck my socks and call me Susie!

Len Ross, North Bay, Ontario

9. Well, blow me down and cast me as a Munchkin.
• This is a movie-wise variant of "blow me down and call me Shorty."

246. SYMPATHY
1. I'd feel for you but I can't reach you.

247. TALLNESS
1. First man: How tall are you?
   Second man: Five feet eleven inches.
   First man: I didn't know they could make a column of shit that high stand upright.

Ted Brown, North Vancouver, British Columbia

248. TALENT
1. Yeah, yeah, they're a very talented family. After the second kid, she threw her afterbirth on the delivery table and the god-damn thing could tap dance.

• The envious neighbour of a prominent Ontario show-biz family spouted this zingy dart of malice.

249. TEA

1. The tea was so weak, you could read the Lord's Prayer through forty fathoms of it.

Lloyd Candow, Pasadena, Newfoundland

2. This brew ain't weak, it's helpless.

Len Ross, North Bay, Ontario

250. TEETH

1. He flosses with a baseball bat.

• This is said of someone who has lost front teeth in a street fight, sports foofaraw, accident, or general donnybrook. In the late 1970s, sportscasters applied it to Bobby Clarke after he lost a few teeth in a difference of opinion during a hockey game. The Hockey Hall of Famer and Flin Flon, Manitoba, native was often branded as a proto-goon, but—bottom line—he put the puck in the net. Clarke was one of the greatest face-off players in the history of professional hockey. But his dirty tactics earned him prime spot when The Philadelphia Flyers were branded as the "Broad Street Bullies." Clarke captained the Flyers to three Stanley Cup championships in 1973, 1974, and 1975, and later served as general manager of the

Flyers. But a certain Russian player named Kharlamov probably remembers Clarke for the 1972 Summit series against Russia's Red Army team, one of the epic encounters in international hockey, won 4–3 by Canada. On alleged orders from a coach, Clarke viciously slashed Kharlamov, fractured the Russian's ankle, and made him useless for the whole series.

251. THEFT
1. He's flip-fingered.

252. THINKING
1. Please check your assumptions at the door.
   Ted Brown, North Vancouver, British Columbia

253. THINNESS
1. He's so skinny his navel scratches his spine.

2. Skinny as a toothpick with all the wood shaved off.
   Jim Maunder, Newfoundland

3. There's more fat on Good Friday.

4. If you don't watch out, you're going to fall through your own asshole and strangle on your sphincter.

254. THREATS

1. You're lookin' to spit Chiclets, dude.

• That is, I'm going to knock your teeth out. Chiclets are little white pieces of chewing gum, vaguely toothlike in shape. This is a common mock-threat among young Canadian hockey players. One trusts that it stays "mock" and that they are not embryonic goons acquiring suitable vocabulary for later skull-splintering brawls.

> Heard in the hockey arena in Dunnville, Ontario

2. I'll give you a haircut with a Weed-Eater.

> Dave Silverthorne, Dunnville, Ontario

3. I will kick your ass so hard you will have to undo your shirt collar to take a dump.

4. I'll nail your nuts to a stump and push you over backwards

> Len Ross, North Bay, Ontario

5. I'll hit you so hard I'll bounce you into the middle of next week.

> Ted Brown, North Vancouver, British Columbia

6. You'll get your head in a fist.

• You are about to get punched on the head. This is still heard in the Ottawa Valley.

> Sarah Elvidge, Yarmouth, Nova Scotia

7. I'll climb up your long skinny frame and gallop your guts out with my toenails!

8. I'm going to have to open a giant, economy-sized can of Whoop-Ass.
•   That is, I'm going to kick your ass good, dude. Originally this is a dialectic variant of "whip your ass" or "whup your ass" which was a physical act performed to punish underlings, servants, and slaves. Movies often show only the shirt being removed before the hapless victim suffered punitive whipping, sometimes with a cat-o-nine-tails. But diaries and eyewitness accounts of public whippings from the seventeenth and eighteenth centuries describe male victim's clothes being ripped completely off, so that the buttocks as well as the back would be slashed with whip wounds. In volume two of *Canadian Sayings*, I listed a variant using "kick-ass" as the punishment.

> Ray Bélanger, St. John's, Newfoundland,
> and other correspondents

9. I'm going to slap a fart out of you that'll whistle like a train on a long grade.

10. You're breeding a scab.
•   You are asking for a fight and a blow that will break the skin.

11. I'm going to kick a mud rut in you and then stomp it dry.

12. I'll slap you so hard your grandchildren will feel it.
•   This implies the injury will be so grievous that inheritable genetic damage may result.

13. You're a booger in the nose of life and the big sneeze is coming.

14. First person: Got a match?
Second person: Yeah, my ass and your face.

   The Billingsley Family, McGregor, Ontario

15. Get bent.
•   This insult, usually from one male to another, is a reference to performing oral sex.

255. TIGHTNESS
1. As tight as a frog's lips around a bus.
•   This is not about the adjective *tight* as synonymous with cheap. This is physical tightness and there are obvious sexual connotations too.

   Denis Tremblay, Ontario

256. TIME

1. How long has it been here? Since Christ was a cowboy.

Harold and Sharon Millie, Pilot Butte, Saskatchewan

257. TOAST

1. Long may your big jig blow!
• This means "Good luck!" in Newfoundland and other maritime locales wherever in the world that sailors speak English. The jib is a triangular sail affixed usually to the foremast and the bowsprit or to its own jib boom. A smaller vessel like a schooner can extricate itself from many nautical troubles if the jib holds. A variant is: Long may your big jib draw. The expression is British in origin and is several hundred years old.

258. TOO MUCH OF A GOOD THING

1. Like a German shepherd fucking a Chihuahua.

259. TRANSPORTATION

1. That guy rides a rice rocket.
• He uses a Suzuki motorcycle or other Japanese-made vehicle.

2. Dude's in a loser cruiser.
• This is Prairie lingo for a minivan.

260. TRAVEL CONDITIONS
1. The road is slicker than deer guts on a doorknob.

261. TROUBLE
1. Wading dick-deep in meadow muffins.
• Although this implies a literal steeping in wet cow manure, the suggestion is that trouble has arrived and knocked loudly on your front door.

   Len Ross, North Bay, Ontario

2. I got more troubles than a woodpecker with chapped lips.

3. Momma told me there'd be days like this, but she never told me there'd be so many and they'd be so close together.

4. If you're short of trouble, take a goat!
• This nugget of proverbial wisdom originated in Finland.

262. TRUST

1. I could get a good look at a T-bone steak by sticking my head up a bull's ass, but I'd rather take the butcher's word for it.

263. TRUTH

1. Does Harvey make hamburgers?

264. TYPISTS

1. Keyboarding with our forehead again, are we? Now, now.

265. UGLINESS

1. The doctor took one look at him after his birth and told his mother, "If this doesn't start to cry in ten seconds, it was a uterine tumour!"

2. He's so ugly, they tied him to flotsam in Halifax Harbour, but even the tide won't take him out.

3. Eyes like piss-holes in snow.
- This may also denote weariness or being hungover.
    Len Ross, North Bay, Ontario

4. She's so ugly, when she phoned a gigolo, he dialled 911.

5. He's no parlour piece.
• The parlour in Canadian homes of fifty to a hundred years ago was a special sitting room set aside for Sunday visitors, for anniversaries, and for funerals. Dead relatives were laid out in their coffins in the parlour. Of course, its origin is slightly more elevated as a room where persons of refinement might speak. The word harks back ultimately to the French verb *parler* 'to speak.'

6. What a scrag! I wouldn't screw her with Fred's dick.
• Perhaps the lady shares this odiously expressed physical revulsion? Or perhaps she wonders precisely how the speaker gained such free access to Frederick's virile apparatus?

7. Last time I saw a mouth like that, it had a hook in it.

Len Ross, North Bay, Ontario

8. Her husband is so ugly a cannibal took one look at him and ordered salad.

9. I wouldn't take her to a dogfight if she was fighting.

10. His face looks like a hawk's arse in a power dive.

11. He had a head on him like a Finlander's dick.
• This was heard in Alberta from a rough and ready oil worker. While it may make sense to a Finnish person, your humble author has no idea what is meant. Perhaps an informative Finn can fill me in?

12. Ugly as a plate of mortal sins.

13. Now don't he look like a piece of straw hanging out of a pig's arse?
   Hal B. O'Neil, Edmonton, Alberta

14. Beauty might be skin deep, but ugly goes right to the bone.

15. Pink as a rooster's dink and cow-shit brown to boot.

16. Last time I saw legs like that they were standing in low water holding up antlers.

17. Had a head on him like a festered foreskin.
   Len Ross, North Bay, Ontario

18. Throw him in a pond and you could skim "ugly" off it for two weeks.

19. He's so ugly, when he was a baby, his parents had a sign in the back window of their car that read: "THING ON BOARD."

20. She's so ugly, when two guys broke into her apartment, she yelled "Rape!" and they yelled back "No fucking way."

21. She's so ugly they threw her away and kept the afterbirth.

22. He is so ugly, when he played in the sandbox, the cat kept covering him up.

266. UNCLEANLINESS
1. I called her up for phone sex and she gave me an ear infection.

267. UNCONCERN
1. If I gave a shit, she'd be the first one I gave it to.

268. UNCOUTH
1. She fell off the potato wagon.

269. UNPLEASANT WOMEN

1. She walks like she has broom rash.
- In other words, she's a bitch and a witch.

2. She had a kick-starter on her broom.

270. UNSTEADINESS

1. Wobbles like a marble in a piss-pot.

Nick Smith, Manitoba

271. UNTRUSTWORTHY

1. When you're not looking, he'll give it to you where the buffalo got the spear.

2. I wouldn't trust you alone in a urinal with a straw.

272. UPTIGHTNESS

1. She's a buckle-arsed shit-squeezer.
- The lady may be of the anal-retentive persuasion.

273. USELESSNESS

1. Ah, sell it!
- In Winnipeg's North End, this once popular

expression was used for something that was no good, useless, or disagreeable.

Matthew Pesclovitch, Winnipeg

2. He should be fed to the pigs while his bones are still soft.
- This is said of a persistently lazy child on the farm.

Dawn Rusnak, Delhi, Ontario

3. You're a fly in a tornado.

4. Useless as a eunuch in a whorehouse.

5. Useless as a chocolate fireguard.

6. Useless as striptease at a nudist camp.

Rex Summersides

7. You are about as much use as a chocolate teapot.

8. Useless as a fart in a windstorm.

Ted Brown, North Vancouver, British Columbia

274. VERMIN
1. Bothered and buggered with bag bugs.
- Bag bugs in Northern Ontario lumber-camp slang are body lice, but not, apparently, bedbugs. Thus a hapless sleeper could be beset with bedbugs and bag

bugs, all of them bad bugs. Now say that quickly, class, while holding your lucky picture of Dalton McGuinty.

275. VIRTUE
1. Rays of pure sunshine pour out her arse.
• The lady is a certified goody-goody, or imagines she is.

276. WAGES
1. This won't buy the baby's boots or pay for the ones she's wearing.
• In other words, this is poor pay indeed. Candace Holmstrom remembers fondly this saying of her late father, Floyd Holmstrom of Winnipeg.

277. WAITERS & WAITRESSES
1. Recently I dined at a trendy Toronto café. I asked the young guy waiting tables if he enjoyed his work. He answered, "Totally! This is the fulfillment of a life goal. After all, I completed four years of Pre-Waiter at York University."

278. WASTING TIME
1. Kicking soft shit.

279. WEARINESS

1. My hole's out.

Len Ross, North Bay, Ontario

280. WEATHER

CLEAR NIGHT

1. The stars are as hard as diamonds.
• This describes a velvet-black, crystal-clear night in any season of the year.

COLD

1. The mercury's hiding this morning.
• "There's a saying used to describe a cold, cold Manitoba morning," writes Bill Turner of Brandon. "Some early thermometers were made in the U.S. or England where their winters were milder and manufacturers there saw no need to take the scale too far below zero. Thus, on some thermometers the mercury would actually drop out of sight behind the thermometer bracket or frame."

2. Cold as a harp seal's nuts.

3. Colder than a stepmother's kiss.

4. Colder than a frog in a frozen pool.

5. Colder than charity and that's some chilly.

6. So cold I had to stick my thumb up my arse to get my pecker long enough to pee.
• Drew Smith of Toronto writes, "I first heard this saying on Conception Bay in Newfoundland spoken by a Nova Scotian sea captain. It describes the weather on an extremely cold morning and the effects of the cold on a particular trip to sea that resulted in us being trapped by ice."

7. Shivering like a dog shitting razor blades.

8. It was so cold in that Saskatchewan town they changed its name to Witch's Tit.
    Christopher Melsted, Banff, Alberta

DRY SPELL
1. So dry on the prairie a few trees are bribing dogs.

FAIR WEATHER OR SUNSHINE
1. *Le soleil est plus beau que moi aujourd'hui.*
• The sun is more beautiful than me today. People say this when they get too much sun in their eyes and they have to squint.

2. *Il y a assez de bleu dans le ciel pour faire des culottes à un irlandais.*
• There's enough blue sky to make an Irishman some

britches. "My grandmother used to say this when we weren't sure if it was gonna rain or not," emails Carmen P. Joynt of Nanaimo, British Columbia. "When there was quite a bit of blue in the sky, it meant that there was a good chance it wouldn't rain."

FORECASTING

1. Do you know the ancient aboriginal way of predicting a long winter? Never mind fat squirrels burying walnuts and acorns. See how much wood the white man has piled in his barn.

HOT

1. So hot a dog and a cat were chasing each other and they were walking.

2. It would melt the snot in your nose.
    Martin Cristopher, Springside, Saskatchewan

3. Hotter than the hammers of Hell.

4. Hotter than a whore's ass on a Saturday night.
• This saying was current in the 1950s among sailors in the Canadian Navy, who presumably were well-qualified to pronounce on this subject.

5. Hotter'n two rats fuckin' in a wool sock.

HOT & SWEATY

1. I've got enough lather in the crack of my ass to shave a porcupine.

HUMIDITY

1. It's closer than Canucks to the border.
•   The humidity is high; one can "feel" the "thick" air close to one's skin. Most Canadians live as far south as possible, in a long band of population stretching from ocean to ocean just north of the American border.

RAIN

1. If there are no clouds over North Vancouver it is going to rain. If there are clouds over North Vancouver it is raining.

Ted Brown, North Vancouver, British Columbia

2. Do you think the rain will hurt the buckwheat if it's done up in cans?
•   On the farm the weather is a constant topic of conversation, sometimes too constant. This is a gently sarcastic response when one has been asked too often about the weather. Once a widespread saying, this particular version was collected in Southern Ontario from Haldimand County farm folk.

SNOW

1. That wind is blowing off snow.
• In other words, it's a cold breeze in late fall, and meaning that a first snowfall is imminent.

Steve McCabe, Oakville, Ontario

2. It's snowing asshole deep to a tall Indian.
• This offensive saying belongs to a less tolerant past, one hopes.

SPRING

1. Spring's here; gophers are out; so are the salesmen.
• Every spring the Manitoba machinery dealers send their salesmen out to start calling on farmers looking for prospective sales.

J.L. Winters, Oak Lake, Manitoba

2. A peck of March dust is worth a king's ransom.

3. A weeping May and a warm June
Makes the farmer whistle a merry tune.

STORMS

1. The storm was so bad, Baba threw the broom out.
• Chris Melsted of Banff writes, "My Ukrainian great-grandmother surprised us always when she would toss her broom out her front door during a really violent Prairie thunderstorm. This superstition

goes back to the old country." Presumably the broom would sweep away the bad weather? I ask any Ukrainian reader who knows the folk reason behind the action to write or email me an explanation.

WIND
1. Windy as a sackful of assholes.

WINTER
1. "An old school teacher of mine used to say that you could always tell the severity of a winter blizzard by how many times you had to go through the ashtrays looking for butts before they got the road open and you could get to town for tobacco."

   Bill Turner, Brandon, Manitoba

Winter—Mild
1. A hornets' nest high in the trees
   Means wintertime will be a breeze.

2. A first snow on unfrozen ground
   Means winter will not stick around.

Winter—Severe
1. When fruit trees bloom late in fall,
   Then winter will not end at all.

281. WEDDINGS

1. A wedding ring is like a tourniquet. It stops your circulation.

Steve McCabe, Oakville, Ontario

282. WEEPING

1. I cried so much I didn't have to pee for a week.

Brendan J. O'Byrne, Regina, Saskatchewan

283. WINDING ROADS

1. The road was so crooked you could see your own tail light.

284. WINNING

1. We won like Wolfe.
• Yeah, some victory. The saying is ironic. We won the battle but our leader died. On September 13, 1759, at the Battle of the Plains of Abraham, Major General James Wolfe commanded a British force that attacked the French under Lieutenant General the Marquis de Montcalm. Wolfe's troops climbed the cliffs below the Plains of Abraham and attacked. The battle was short and Quebec surrendered a few days later. Both Montcalm and Wolfe died of their wounds. We won like Wolfe and now we can stay calm like Montcalm. Or maybe not.

285. WISHING

1. Go ahead, wish. If a frog had wings, it wouldn't bump its ass.

286. WORK

1. I'm going to fuck the dog and sell the puppies.

•   A correspondent who wishes to remain anonymous writes: "When I was working on the DEW Line more than twenty years ago, I heard this variation from a worker who was bragging that he was laying back that day. Some would be offended; they'd call the saying species-ist."

The DEW Line stood for Distant Early Warning Line, a chain of sixty-three radar and communication systems stretching 3,000 miles from the northwest coast of Alaska to the eastern shore of Baffin Island opposite Greenland. The DEW Line grew out of fifties Cold War paranoia. It sprang from a detailed examination made by scientists in 1952 at the Summer Study Group at the Massachusetts Institute of Technology. Their subject was the vulnerability of the United States and Canada to air attack by the Soviet Union. Their recommendation was that a Distant Early Warning Line be built across our Arctic border as rapidly as possible. The complete operating radar system across the top of North America with its own dependable communications network began operation in July 1957. The DEW Line extends east and west at roughly the 69th parallel. On the average, it is about 200 miles north of the Arctic Circle and 1,400 miles from the North Pole.

2. Stuke or ride the binder.
• In other words, do something or get the hell out of the way. Steve McCabe of Oakville who was brought up on a rural Ontario farm writes, "This expression comes from lazy or tired field workers catching a ride on the binder in the earlier days of baling hay or straw. The good worker was the one stuking (piling) the bales."

3. Now we're sucking diesel.
• This modern Irish saying implies that we are making progress.

4. She's going to ride that doorknob until her tits fall off.
• That is, she's just jerking around in an idle, masturbatory manner and not really working on the assigned project.

5. Gentlemen, balls to the wall.
• That is, we're going to be working hard right down to the last minute.

6. Cake and pie.

• Related to a piece of cake and a piece of pie, this Australian expression refers to an easy job. This brings to my mind the crafty film director Alfred Hitchcock confronted with a pompous film critic wondering about verisimilitude in Hitchcock's films. Said the portly director, almost always brighter than his interviewers, "Some people's stories are slices of life. My stories are slices of cake." If only the mournful-buttocked squad of Canadian authors of "the high seriousness," those glum-bummed pomposities who parade across the remainder bins with their dreary tales of lumberjacks who accidentally chop off their own dicks and moose that contract leprosy, if only those uppity snooze-inducers could partake of Hitchcock's humility, we readers of Canadian novels would all be freer of ennui and free also of the sallow glaze of boredom that bedims the reading eye when the second chapter of a Canadian novel begins, "Mom died that night on the tractor, while she was ploughing the back forty and Dad was ploughing Olga, the hired man's wife, in the barn."

7. Locked and loaded.
• On the point of beginning any difficult task, the joker will twist his baseball cap ninety degrees so that the visor portion is over one ear and say, "Locked and loaded."

Denis Tremblay, Ontario

8. It kicks the green Jesus out of working.
• This little blast of blasphemy describes any activity other than work.

9. Slick as cat shit on glass.
• Devon Brown writes that this was "used by my father to describe anything that is accomplished easily." It's still heard in the Annapolis Valley in Nova Scotia.

10. His balls are on the chopping block.
• He is ultimately responsible for his actions at work with the risk of getting fired.

11. Don't just stand there with one thumb in your ear and one in your ass waiting for someone to holler "Change!"
• From an Edmonton steel mill, this is an injunction to get on with the job.

12. Hop short now!
• This Ottawa Valley expression means "wise up, move fast."

> Sarah Elvidge, Yarmouth, Nova Scotia

13. A man was given a job impossible in his estimation to accomplish. His response: I'll get right

to that, soon as I finish stuffing this freight train up this snake's arsehole.

T. Wolfe, Pense, Saskatchewan

14. Give Gran an axe for Xmas.
•   The implication is you gift a person with something that will only make them work harder.

15. You're a pimple on the prick of progress.
•   You are not trying to fit in with the new plans here at the factory.

16. We pretend to work because they pretend to pay us.
•   This peevish, whining complaint originated among Russian Communist factory workers in the 1950s. Since the early 1960s it's been a staple joke of English Canadian union meetings. By the way, there will be no more cheap Russian jokes in this book. Does the name Pavlov ring a bell?

287. YES IS THE ANSWER.

1. Q: You up for another beer?
    A: Does a duck with a big dick drag weeds?
•   "A close friend of mine, Happy Cam, from the Peace River area brought this saying down to

Edmonton. I would like to think this saying is now as popular in Edmonchuk as it is up north. There you have it! An Alberta classic!" writes Richard Wirsta of Edmonton.

2. Does Pinocchio have wooden nuts?

• On that high-class scrotal note, I think Uncle Billy will close this third volume of sayings used by Canadians. There shall be a fourth volume if readers send in new and old Canadian expressions not yet in print. Thanks again to the readers who supplied the funniest sayings in this collection. If these wonderful old saws gave you a chuckle and made you remember a couple of Canadian folk doozies that are not in the first three books, then please send them to me by mail or email. Do give the circumstance and location in Canada when you first heard the saying. And perhaps your name will appear in the fourth volume of *Canadian Sayings*? Please note in the email address that canadiansayings is all one word and all lower case, and mountaincable is all one word and lower case. You may also use my website to submit sayings.

Bill Casselman,
205 Helena Street,
Dunnville, Ontario, Canada
N1A 2S6
email: canadiansayings@mountaincable.net
website: www.billcasselman.com

MORE BILL CASSELMAN BOOKS
ABOUT CANADIAN WORDS
FROM McARTHUR & COMPANY

CASSELMAN'S CANADIAN WORDS

In this #1 Best-Seller, Bill Casselman delights and startles with word stories from every province and territory of Canada. Did you know that *Scarborough* means "Harelip's Fort"? The names of *Lake Huron & Huronia* stem from a vicious, racist insult. Huron in old French meant 'long-haired clod.' French soldiers labelled the Wendat people with this nasty misnomer in the 1600s. *To deke out* is a Canadian verb that began as hockey slang, short for 'to decoy an opponent.' Canada has a fish that ignites. On our Pacific coast, the oolichan or *candlefish* is so full of oil it can be lighted at one end and used as a candle. "*Mush! Mush!* On, you huskies!" cried Sergeant Preston of The Yukon to 1940s radio listeners, thus introducing a whole generation of Canucks to the word once widely used in the Arctic to spur on sled dogs. Although it might sound like a word from Inuktitut, early French trappers first used it, borrowing the term from the Canadian French command to a horse to go: *Marche! Marche!* Yes, it's Québécois for giddyap!

All these and more fascinating terms from Canadian place names, politics, sports, plants and animals, clothing. Everything from Canadian monsters to mottoes is here.

CASSELMAN'S CANADIAN WORDS
ISBN 1-55278-034-1
224 pages, illustrated

CASSELMANIA
MORE WACKY CANADIAN WORDS & SAYINGS

Should you purchase a copy of *Casselmania*? Below, dear reader, is a quiz to try. If you pass, buy *Casselmania*. If you fail, buy two copies!

1. "Slackers" is a nickname for what Canadian city?
(a) Vancouver
(b) Halifax
(c) Sackville, New Brunswick
ANSWER: (b). Why "Slackers"? Because often when Canadian Navy crews put in to Halifax harbour, the sailors had some "slack" time for shore leave.

2. *Eh?* is a true marker of Canadian speech. But which of the following authors uses *eh?* exactly as Canadians now use it?
(a) Emily Brontë in *Wuthering Heights*.
(b) Charles Dickens in *Bleak House*.
(c) Geoffrey Chaucer in The Canterbury Tales in AD 1400.
ANSWER: All of the above! *Eh?* is almost 1,000 years old as an interjection in Old English, Middle English, and, of course, in modern Canadian English too.

3. The first *Skid Row* or *Skid Road* in Canada was in Vancouver at the end of the 19th century. The term originated because:
(a) Alcoholics kept slipping in the muddy streets
(b) Out-of-work loggers drank in cheap saloons at the end of a road used to skid logs
(c) Cheap houses were moved on skids to slummy areas
ANSWER: (b). Skids were greased logs used to slide rough timber to a waterway or railhead. There was a skid road in Vancouver, where unemployed loggers waited for jobs, and took the odd bottle of liquid refreshment.

CASSELMANIA
MORE WACKY CANADIAN WORDS & SAYINGS
ISBN 1-55278-035-X
298 pages, illustrated

CANADIAN GARDEN WORDS

Trowel in hand, Bill Casselman digs into the loamy lore and fascinating facts about how we have named the plants that share our Dominion. But are there *Canadian* Garden Words? Yes! Try those listed below.

Camas Lily is a bulb grown all over the world for its spiky blue flowers. The name arose in British Columbia where First Peoples cooked and ate the bulbs. Camas means 'sweet' in Nootka, a Pacific Coast language. The original name of Victoria on Vancouver Island was Camosun, in Nootka 'place where we gather camas bulbs.'

A Snotty Var is a certain species of fir tree in Newfoundland. Why? Find out in *Canadian Garden Words.*

Mistletoe! So Christmassy. The word means 'poop on a stick.' Oops! Look within for a bounty of surprising origins of plant names. Orchid means 'testicle' in Greek. So does avocado. While plant names have come into English from dozens of world languages, Bill Casselman has found the Canadian connection to 100s of plant names and garden lore and packed this book with them. Casselman reports on Canadian plant names and on the origin of all the common trees and flowers that decorate our gardens from Fogo Island to Tofino, B.C.

CANADIAN GARDEN WORDS
ISBN 1-55278-036-8
356 pages, illustrated

CANADIAN FOOD WORDS
THE JUICY LORE AND TASTY ORIGINS OF FOODS
THAT FOUNDED A NATION

* Winner Gold Medal Culinary Book of the Year Award for 1999 from Cuisine Canada

"A glorious, informative, and funny collection of
food-related definitions and stories!"
—Marion Kane, food editor, *Toronto Star*

"Even readers who are unlikely to fry a doughnut in seal
blubber oil will enjoy this latest romp by writer and
broadcaster Bill Casselman . . . he mixes in so much
entertaining information and curious Canadian lore."
—Books, *Globe & Mail*

Do you know that fine Canadian dish, Son-of-a-Bitch-in-a-Sack? It's a real Alberta chuck wagon pudding. In this fully illustrated, 304-page romp, Bill tells the amusing stories behind such hearty Canadian fare as *gooeyducks* and *hurt pie*. The juicy lore and tangy tales of foods that founded a nation are all here: from *scrunchins* to *rubbaboo*, from *bangbelly* to *poutine*, from *Winnipeg jambusters* to *Nanaimo bars*, from *Malpeque oysters* to *nun's farts!* If you think foods of Canadian origin are limited to pemmican and pea soup, you need to dip your ladle into the bubbling kettle of *Canadian Food Words*.

CANADIAN FOOD WORDS
THE JUICY LORE AND TASTY ORIGINS OF FOODS
THAT FOUNDED A NATION
ISBN 1-55278-018-X
304 pages, illustrated

CANADIAN SAYINGS

1,200 FOLK SAYINGS USED BY CANADIANS
Collected & Annotated by Bill Casselman

62 weeks on The National Post Top Ten Canadian Non-Fiction List!

Samples of Canadian sayings from Bill's best-selling book:

- She's got more tongue than a Mountie's boot.
- That smell would gag a maggot on a gut wagon.
- I've seen more brains in a Manitoba sucked egg.
- He's thicker than a B.C. pine stump.
- Saskatchewan is so flat you can watch your dog run away from home for a week.
- He's so dumb he thinks Medicine Hat is a cure for head lice.
- Sign in bathroom where husband shaves: Warning— Objects in mirror are dumber than they appear.
- Of childish behaviour in a grown man: That boy never did grow up. One day, he just sorta haired over.

There is a reason this book made Canadians chuckle for more than a best-selling year. Buy it and find out why, as you laugh along with what one reviewer called "the funniest Canadian book I've ever read!"

CANADIAN SAYINGS
1,200 FOLK SAYINGS USED BY CANADIANS
Collected & Annotated by Bill Casselman
ISBN 1-55278-076-7
138 pages

WHAT'S IN A CANADIAN NAME?

THE ORIGINS & MEANINGS OF
CANADIAN SURNAMES

From Atwood to Applebaum, from Bobak to Bullard, with Gabereau, Hanomansing, Harnoy, Krall, Tobin, and Shamas tossed into the linguistic salad of our last names, Bill Casselman tells here the fascinating story of surnames, of how humans came to use last names, and of what some last names mean, names that every Canadian knows. Did you know that pop singer Shania Twain bears an Ojibwa first name that means 'on my way'? Movie star Keanu Reeves has a first name that is Hawaiian for 'cool breeze.' Talk show host Mike Bullard's last name is Middle English for 'trickster.' Surnames can trick and surprise you too. Byron sounds sooo uppercrust, doesn't it? Proud family moniker of the famous English poet, etc. Too bad Byron means "at the cowsheds" from Old English *byrum* and suggests a family origin not in a stately home but in a stately stable! More surprises and delights await any Canadian reader interested in genealogy and surnames.

WHAT'S IN A CANADIAN NAME?
THE ORIGINS & MEANINGS OF CANADIAN SURNAMES
ISBN 1-55278-141-0
250 pages

CANADIAN SAYINGS 2

"Bill Casselman, bluenose among schooners on the sea
of popular etymology, moors his mighty vessel,
nets a-teeming with Canadian words."
—Indigo Internet review

Canada's funniest collector of salty sayings is back! He's got
more than 1,000 new sayings used by Canadians, expressions
not in the first volume of Canadian Sayings. As usual, Bill has
been careful about the limits of good taste. So you'll find old
saws like these:

- We were so poor, we never had decorations on the
  Christmas tree unless Grandpa sneezed.
- Tongue-tied? That dude couldn't adlib a fart at a bean
  supper.
- The gene pool around here could use a little chlorine.

Yes, Casselman keeps his customary firm grip on decorum
and refinement by such offerings as this:

- Toronto woman to her girlfriend at a trendy café: "Sure,
  I understand about premature ejaculation, but I've been
  vaccinated slower than that."

Would some of these sayings make a corpse blush? The
author sincerely hopes not. But only the reader can tell. So
check out volume 2 right now!

CANADIAN SAYINGS 2
1,000 FOLK SAYINGS USED BY CANADIANS
Newly Collected and Annotated by Bill Casselman
ISBN 1-55278-272-7
170 pages

All Bill Casselman's books are available from online booksellers and at bookstores across Canada.

These Canadian Sayings and 1,000 more wait inside this third volume.

- He's all Stampede hat and no cattle.
- This Alberta put-down is heard throughout the year.

- We've ehed but we ain't shook.
- We have exchanged Canadian comments like "Cold, eh?" but we don't know each other well.

- The Princes' Gates are open.
- Your fly is down. The zipper on your pants is undone. This is something a Toronto parent used to say to a boy. It's probably entirely local to Toronto. The Princes' Gates are the monumental entrance to the Canadian National Exhibition grounds.

- I took my pants off for that?
- The business endeavour or sexual encounter did not prove worthwhile.

- To rock the canoe.
- To see if the beaver still needs the log.
- To pound the tundra checking for permafrost.
- These are Canadian ways of saying 'to make love.'

- Very scary! That's a real turd-curdler.

- She wears a ponytail to cover up the valve stem.

- If I promise to miss you, will you go away?

OTHER BOOKS BY BILL CASSELMAN
FROM McARTHUR & COMPANY

Casselman's Canadian Words

Casselmania

Canadian Garden Words

Canadian Food Words

Canadian Sayings

What's in a Canadian Name?

Canadian Sayings 2